Sight Reading & Rhythm Every Day®

Helen Marlais with Kevin Olson

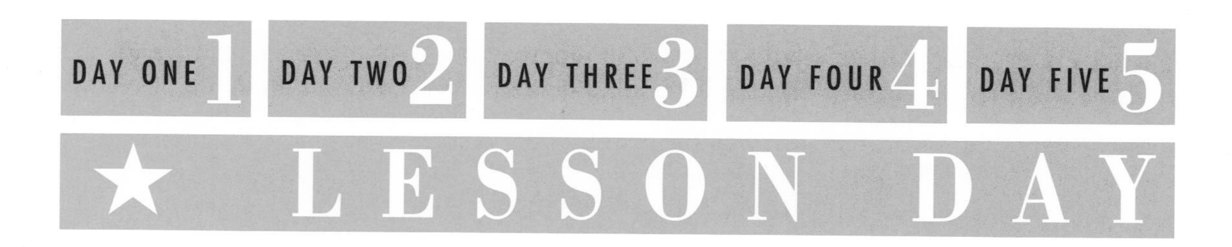

Production: Frank J. Hackinson
Production Coordinators: Joyce Loke and Satish Bhakta
Cover: Terpstra Design, San Francisco
Text Design and Layout: Terpstra Design and Maritza Cosano Gomez
Engraving: Tempo Music Press, Inc.
Printer: Tempo Music Press, Inc.

ISBN 1-56939-732-5

ABOUT THE AUTHORS

Helen Marlais' active performance schedule includes concerts in North America, Western and Eastern Europe, the Middle East, and Asia, and her travels abroad have included performing and teaching at the leading conservatories in Lithuania, Estonia, Italy, France, Hungary, Turkey, Russia, and China. She has performed with members of the Pittsburgh, Minnesota, Grand Rapids, Des Moines, Cedar Rapids, and Beijing National Symphony Orchestras to name a few, and is recorded on Stargrass Records®, Gasparo, and Centaur record labels. She has had numerous collaborative performances broadcast regionally, nationally, and internationally on radio, television, and the Internet with her husband, clarinetist Arthur Campbell. She presents workshops at every national convention and is a featured presenter at state conventions. She has been a guest teacher and performer at leading music schools and conservatories throughout North America, Europe, and Asia. Dr. Marlais is the Director of Keyboard Publications for The FJH Music Company Inc. Her articles can be read in *Keyboard Companion, The American Music Teacher,* and *Clavier* magazines.

Dr. Marlais is an associate professor of piano at Grand Valley State University in Grand Rapids, Michigan, where she directs the piano pedagogy program, coordinates the group piano programs, and teaches studio piano. She received her DM in piano performance and pedagogy from Northwestern University and her MM in piano performance from Carnegie Mellon University. She has also held full-time faculty piano positions at the Crane School of Music, S.U.N.Y. at Potsdam, Iowa State University, and Gustavus Adolphus College. Visit: www.helenmarlais.com.

Kevin Olson is an active pianist, composer, and faculty member at Elmhurst College near Chicago, Illinois, where he teaches classical and jazz piano, music theory, and electronic music. He holds a Doctor of Education degree from National-Louis University, and bachelor's and master's degrees in music composition and theory from Brigham Young University. Before teaching at Elmhurst College, he held a visiting professor position at Humboldt State University in California.

A native of Utah, Kevin began composing at the age of five. When he was twelve, his composition *An American Trainride* received the Overall First Prize at the 1983 National PTA Convention in Albuquerque, New Mexico. Since then, he has been a composer-in-residence at the National Conference on Piano Pedagogy and has written music for the American Piano Quartet, Chicago a cappella, the Rich Matteson Jazz Festival, and several piano teachers associations around the country.

Kevin maintains a large piano studio, teaching students of a variety of ages and abilities. Many of the needs of his own piano students have inspired a diverse collection of books and solos published by The FJH Music Company Inc., which he joined as a writer in 1994.

HOW THE SERIES IS ORGANIZED

All rhythmic activities

All sight-reading activities

All Rhythm Flash!, Pattern Flash!, Interval Flash!, & Chord Flash! activities

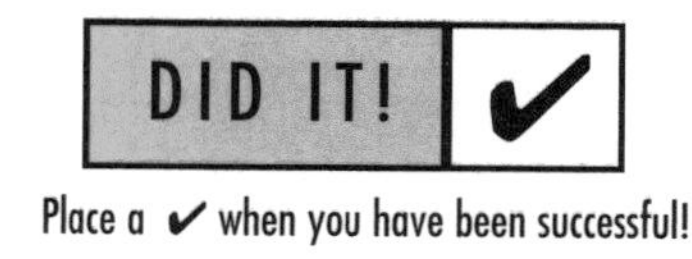

Place a ✔ when you have been successful!

Each unit of the series is divided into five separate days of enjoyable rhythmic and sight-reading activities. Students complete these short daily activities "Every Day" at home, by themselves. Every day the words, "Did It!" are found in boxes for the student to check once they have completed both the rhythm and sight-reading activities.

The new concepts are identified in the upper right-hand corner of each unit. Once introduced, these concepts are continually reinforced through subsequent units.

On the lesson day, there are short rhythmic and sight-reading activities that will take only minutes for the teacher and student to do together. An enjoyable sight-reading duet wraps up each unit.

BOOK 6

Rhythm:

Rhythmic activities in book 6 include the following:

- Internalize rhythms in many ways by clapping, tapping, and stomping on the floor.
- Reinforcement of sixteenth-note patterns:

- Lyrics spoken in rhythm.
- Adding bar lines and correct time signatures to excerpts and then counting the examples out loud.
- Clapping rhythmic examples by memory—an excellent ear training and memory exercise.
- Tapping different rhythms in each hand.
- "Rhythm Flashes"—short rhythmic patterns that students look at briefly and then tap by memory. This skill helps them to think and prepare quickly.

Fingering:

Very little fingering is provided so that students learn to look ahead and think about patterns. They are sometimes asked to decide their own fingering and write it directly in their score before starting to play.

Tips for Sight Reading:

- Decide the time and key signature.
- Look for patterns in the music (intervals, phrases, rhythms).
- Sing or hum the piece in your mind.
- Plan the fingering.
- Make sure you count the rhythm at a steady tempo before starting.
- Plan the sound before you play.

Tips when playing:

- Sight read at a tempo that you can keep steady, without stopping.
- Keep your eyes on the music, not on your hands.
- Play musically and don't worry about mistakes. Concentrate on keeping the tempo.
- Make use of the metronome.

Reading:

Pieces are sight read using dominant seventh chords, first in root position and then in inversion. Students continue to harmonize using traditional cadences in major and minor. Students sight read pieces with diminished and augmented triads. Simple contrapuntal pieces are sight read to help in the study of baroque music, along with identifying melodic and harmonic major and minor intervals. Students are asked to focus on balancing simple melodies over simple accompaniments and play pieces that reinforce parallel and contrasting phrasing. Duet playing as a Lesson Day activity continues to further reinforce the importance of continuity when sight reading.

Major and minor white and black keys are reinforced. Students are asked to transpose short pieces to other keys, continue to harmonize using chord symbols, and play pieces with changing clefs and ledger lines.

Sight-Reading activities include the following:

- "Pattern Flashes," "Chord Flashes," and "Interval Flashes"—short patterns to play or look at briefly and then play by memory, further helping to look ahead and think and prepare quickly.

- Learning to "plan" for note and rhythmic accuracy, correct articulations, and a good sound.
- "Hearing" what the music is supposed to sound like before starting to play.
- Helpful suggestions that guide students to think before playing and not to stop once they have started!
- Singing or humming the melody of some of the excerpts, which encourages listening while maintaining a constant pulse and the forward motion of the musical line.
- Planning intervals, patterns, and crossovers before playing.
- Frequent use of the metronome.

TABLE OF CONTENTS

Sight Reading and Rhythm Review - Let's Get Started!

It's Matching Time!

How well do you know your music? Match the correct definitions to the terms or concepts by writing the letter next to the number.

_____ **1.**

_____ **2.** 

_____ **3.** *dolce*

_____ **4.** 

_____ **5.**

_____ **6.** *sempre*

_____ **7.** *meno*

_____ **8.** ¢

_____ **9.**

_____ **10.**

A. An Italian term that means to play "sweetly."

B. E♭ major

C. An Italian term that means "less."

D. An Italian term that means "always."

E. cut time

F. $\frac{6}{8}$ time

G. E–C–A (going down) in the bass clef.

H. triad and its inversions

I. i-iv$^6_4$-i-V$^6_5$-i cadence in B minor

J. second inversion chords

Answers: 1.–F, 2.–H, 3.–A, 4.–I, 5.–B, 6.–D, 7.–C, 8.–E, 9.–J, 10–G

What is the key? _______ Plan the chords and the fingering before playing.

What is the key? ______ Study the moves before you begin.

Plan all the moves. Then tap the rhythm. Where the ☺ is, add an *allargando* (*allargando* means "to broaden" in Italian).

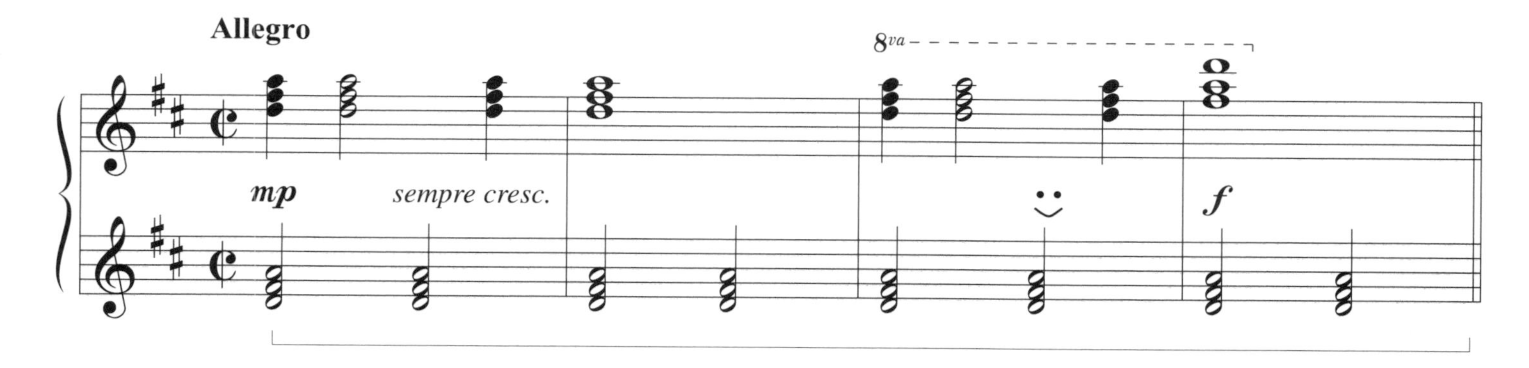

Unit 1

New Concept: sixteenth-note rhythms (♬) in the keys of C, G, and F major. Review of authentic cadences; dominant seventh chords in root position in the keys of C, G, and F major

Rhythm—Add the correct time signature. Clap and count the following rhythm with energy!

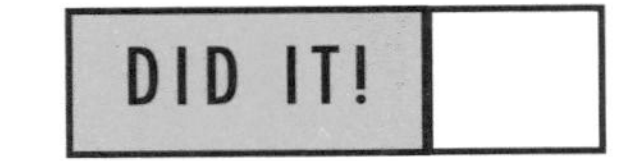

Place a ✔ when you have been successful!

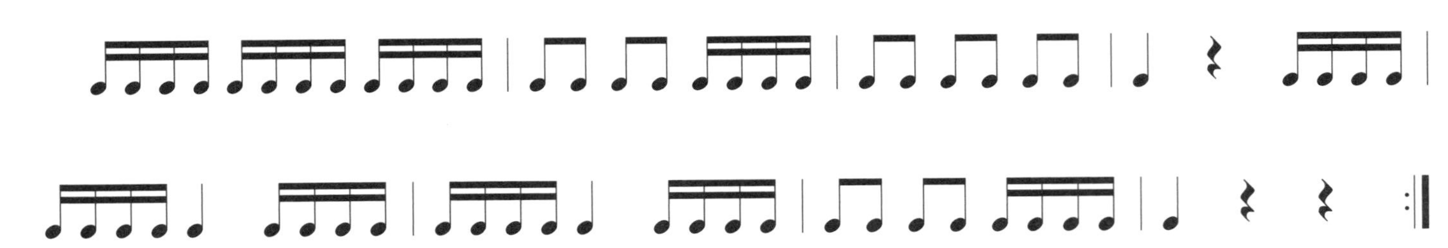

Sight reading—Tips for sight reading:

DID IT!

- Decide the time and key signatures.
- Look for patterns in the music (intervals, phrases, rhythms).
- Sing or hum the piece in your mind.
- Plan the fingering.
- Make sure you count the rhythm at a steady tempo before starting.
- Plan the sound before you play.

Practice the left-hand cadences until comfortable.

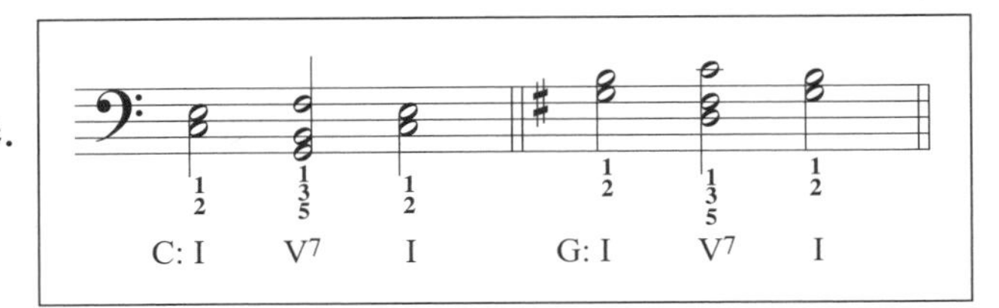

Rhythm Flash!—Clap and count the first example. Close the book—can you clap it from memory? Then try the next example in the same way.

DID IT!

Sight reading—Tips when playing:

DID IT!

- Sight read at a tempo that you can keep steady, without stopping.
- Keep your eyes on the music, and not on your hands.
- Play musically and don't worry about mistakes. Concentrate on keeping the tempo.
- Make use of the metronome.

Silently play this harmonization on the top of the keys, planning the left-hand chords. Pick a tempo you can keep steady.

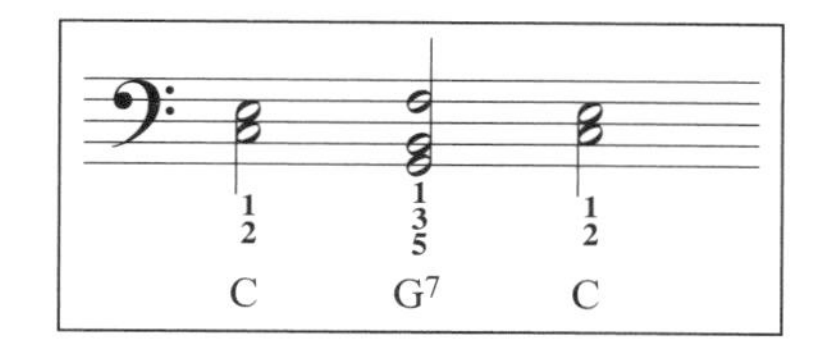

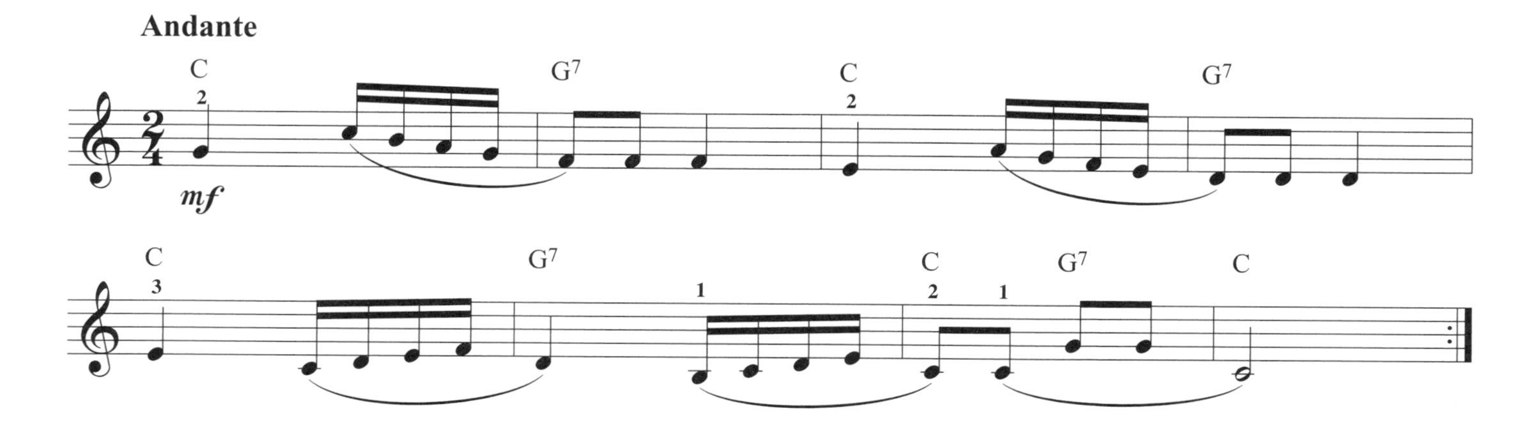

On a scale from 1–5, with 5 being the best, how was your sight reading? _____________

Rhythm—There is one mistake in each example. Fix it, and then clap and count aloud.

Pattern Flash!—Plan pattern No. 1 for 10 seconds. Then play it. Do the same for pattern No. 2. How is it *different* from the first pattern?

DID IT!

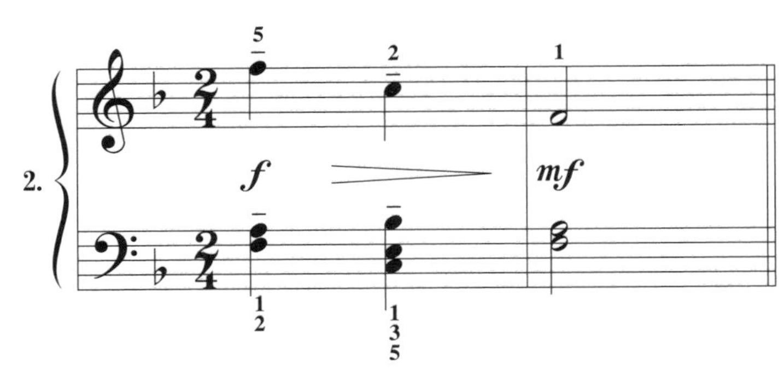

Sight reading—Silently plan this piece hands separately, and then hands together. Tap the rhythm of both hands until comfortable. Once you start, don't stop until the very end!

DID IT!

Transpose to the keys of:

G major _____ C major _____

DAY FOUR

Rhythm—Add bar lines to the following example. Using the metronome at ♪=152, play one note on the piano for the following rhythm and count evenly.

DID IT!

Rhythm Flash!—As quickly as you can, circle all of the patterns that are in $\frac{3}{4}$ time.

DID IT!

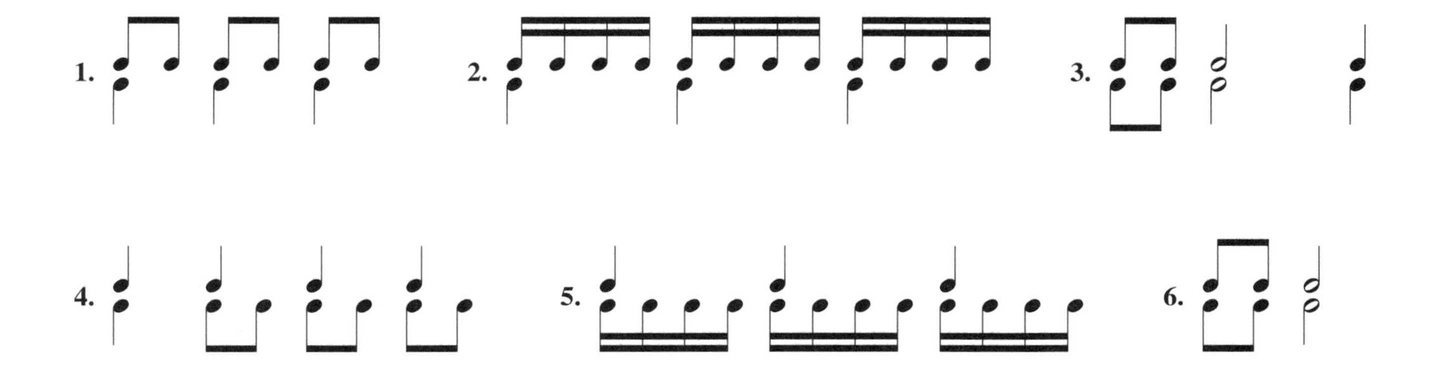

Sight reading—Silently plan this piece hands separately, and then hands together. Then play it at a steady rhythm.

DID IT!

Transpose to the keys of:

A major _____ F major _____ C major _____

Rhythm—With the metronome at ♪=126, clap and count the following rhythm. Then say the words the second time through.

DID IT!

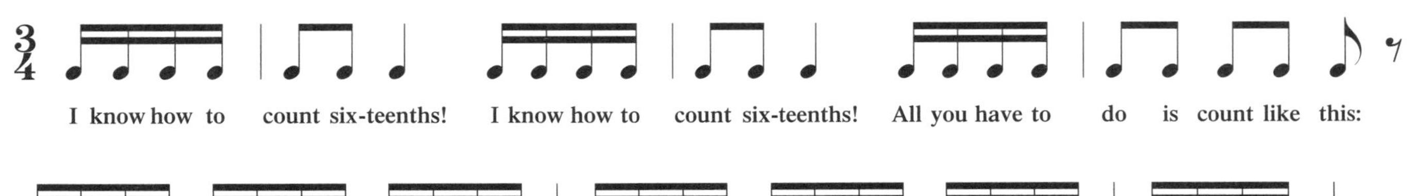

Pattern Flash!—Plan the tonic and dominant harmonies. Be sure to move comfortably from tonic to dominant *without* reaching.

DID IT!

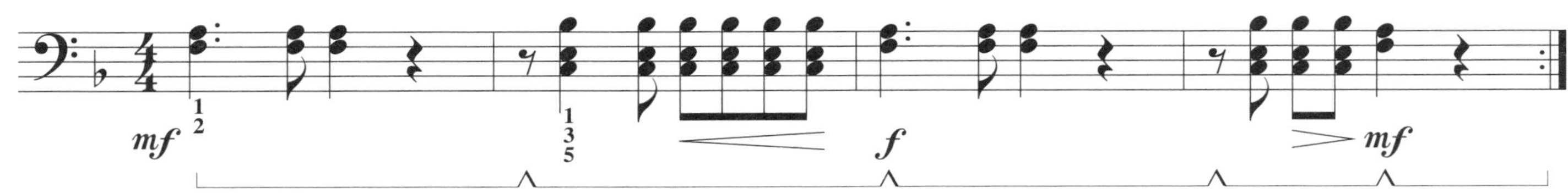

Sight reading—Tap the exercise on your lap, paying special attention to the last measure. Can you "sing" the melody in your mind before playing it?

DID IT!

Ensemble Piece

DID IT!

Before playing, find the G major scales. How are measures 3-4 different than measures 7-8?

Early Morning Practicing

Teacher accompaniment (student plays as written)

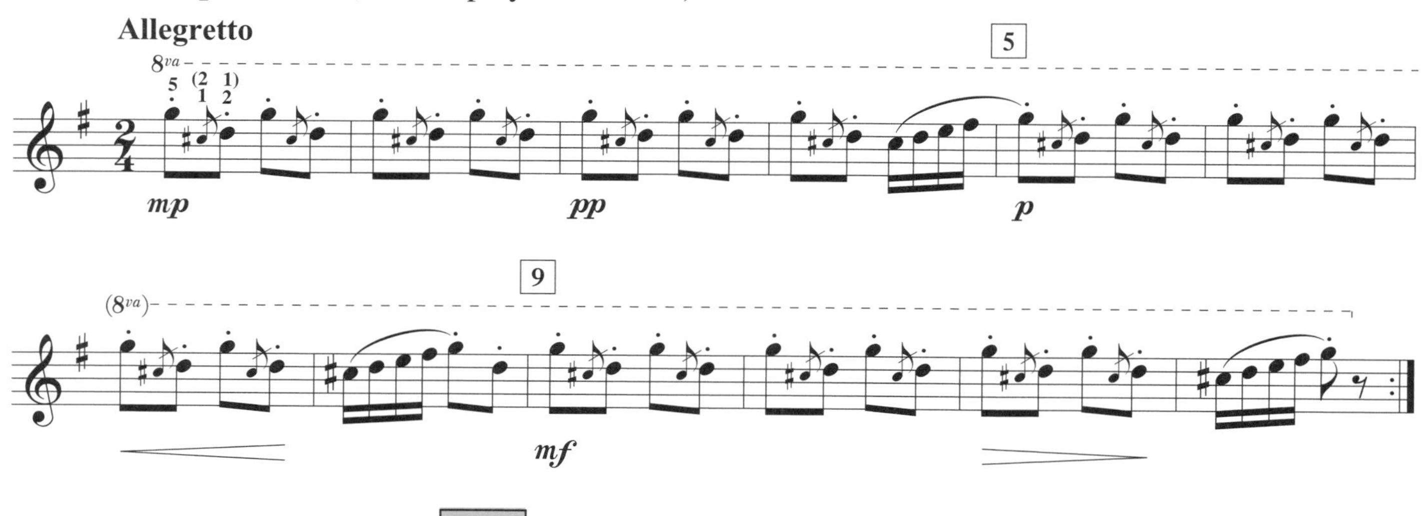

? After playing, ask yourself, "Did I play evenly and did I count?"

Unit 2

DAY ONE

New Concepts: sixteenth-note rhythms (♬♬) in the keys of D, A, E, and B major; intervals of an octave. Review of authentic cadences; dominant seventh chords in root position in the keys of D, A, E, and B major

Rhythm—Clap and count with energy in your voice. *Crescendo* to every downbeat.

DID IT!

Pattern Flash!—Study these two phrases for 5 seconds or less. Then play them while counting.

DID IT!

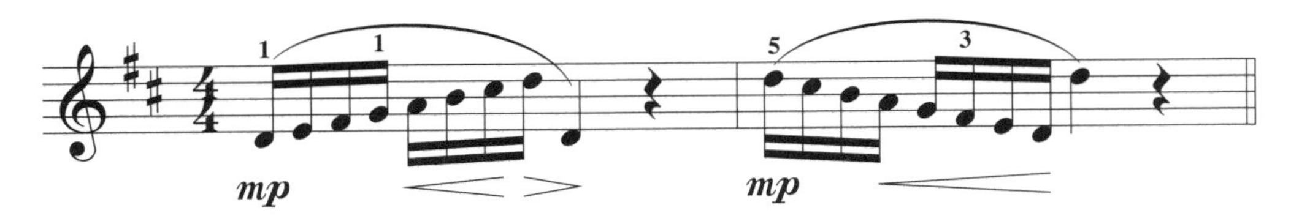

Sight reading—Plan the tonic and dominant chords. Then add the fingering in this piece before playing it.

DID IT!

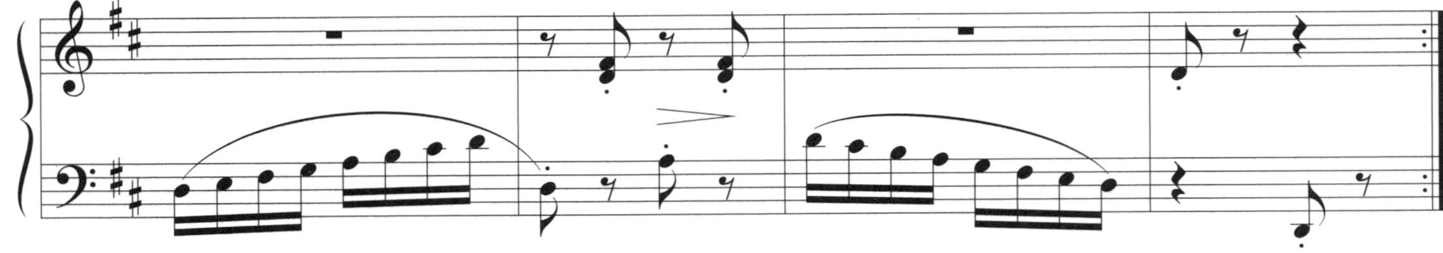

Transpose this piece to the keys of:

E major _____ C major _____ A major _____

Rhythm—There are two mistakes below. Fix them, and then clap and count aloud!

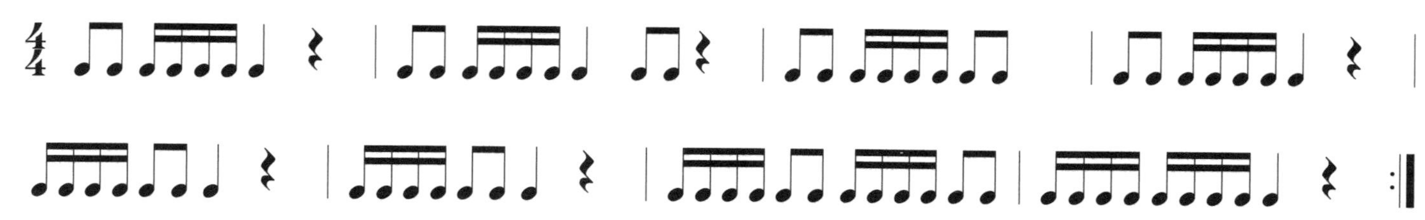

Interval Flash!—Study the rhythm before you begin. Place your fingers over the keys that are sharped. Do not reach for the keys! Name the intervals as you play.

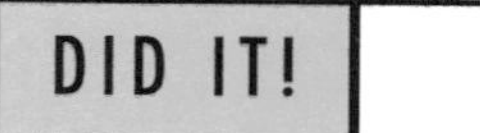

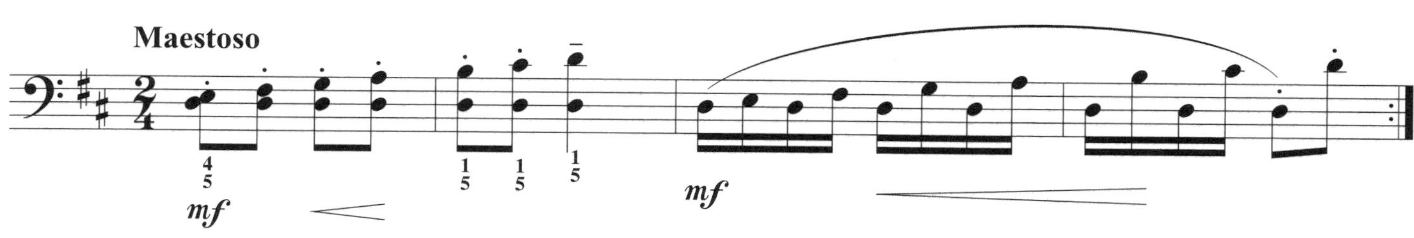

Sight reading—Add the fingering in the left hand. Then tap and count the rhythm hands together. Silently play the piece on the top of the keys. Once you begin, play with confidence until the end!

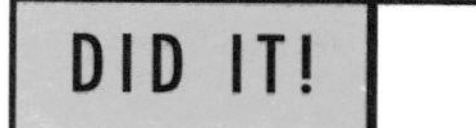

Transpose this piece to the keys of:

A major _____ Key of your choice _____

Rhythm—Add bar lines. Tap the top line with your right hand, snap the middle line with your left hand, and stomp the bottom line with your foot.

DID IT!

Pattern Flash!—Plan the chords.

DID IT!

How are these patterns similar? How are they different?
Can you play them from memory the second time through?

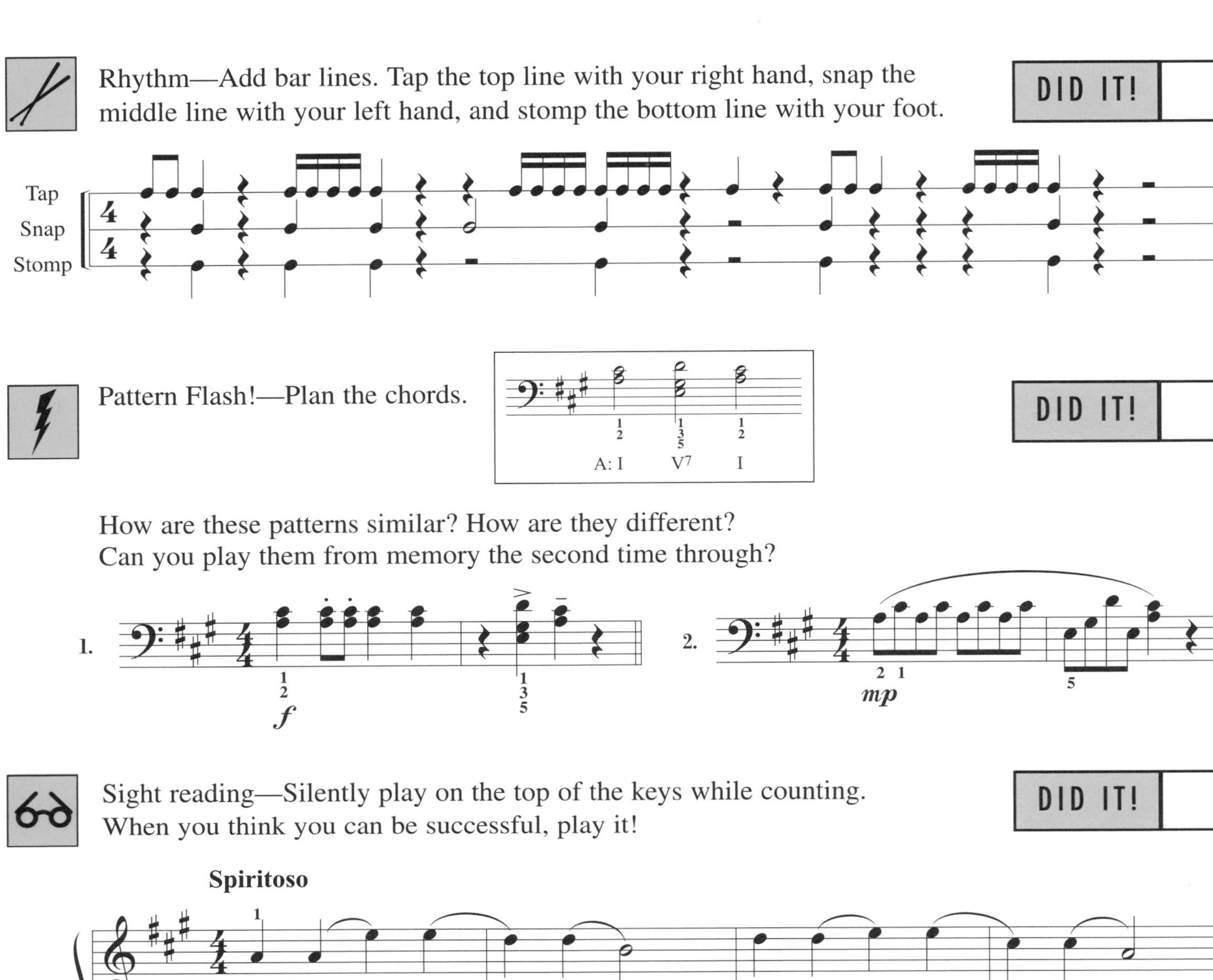

Sight reading—Silently play on the top of the keys while counting.
When you think you can be successful, play it!

DID IT!

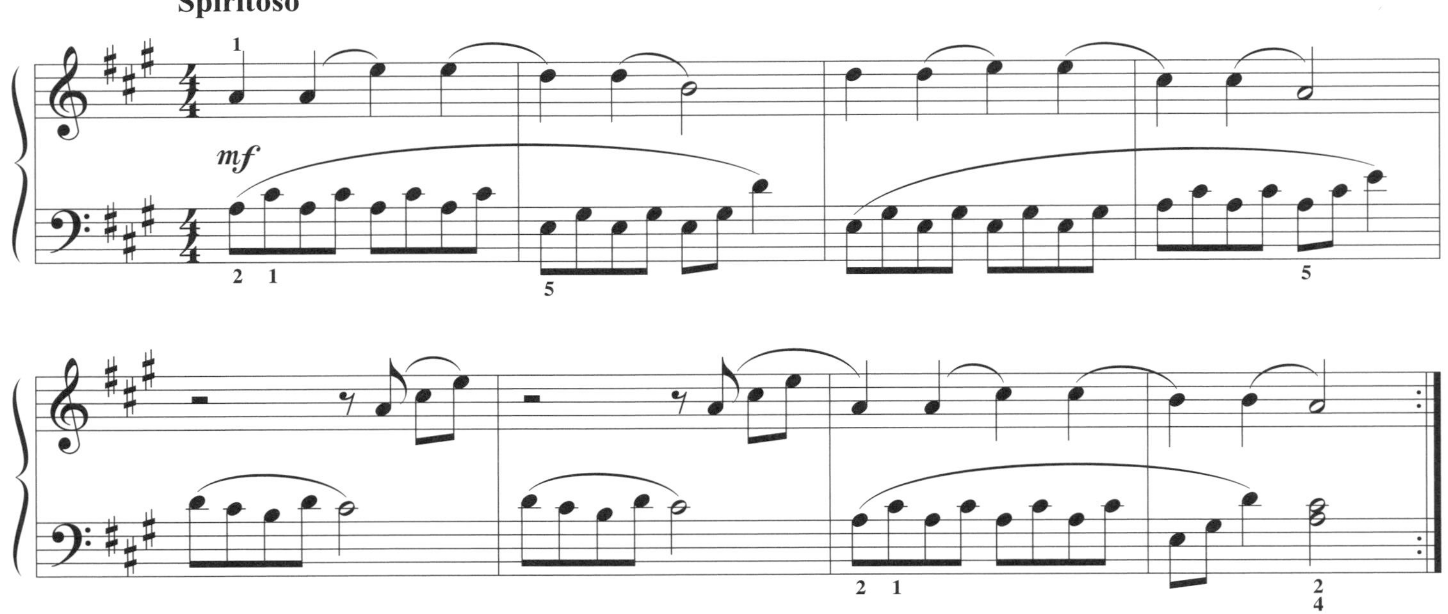

What grade would you give yourself for this sight reading exercise? (circle one) A B C D F

Rhythm—Add the bar lines and the correct time signature.
Then clap and count aloud.

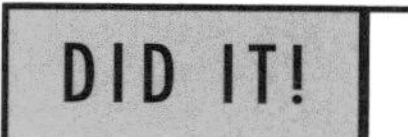

Rhythm Flash!—Add the time signature to each example then tap the rhythms.
Can you accomplish this in less than 10 seconds? Yes, No (circle one)

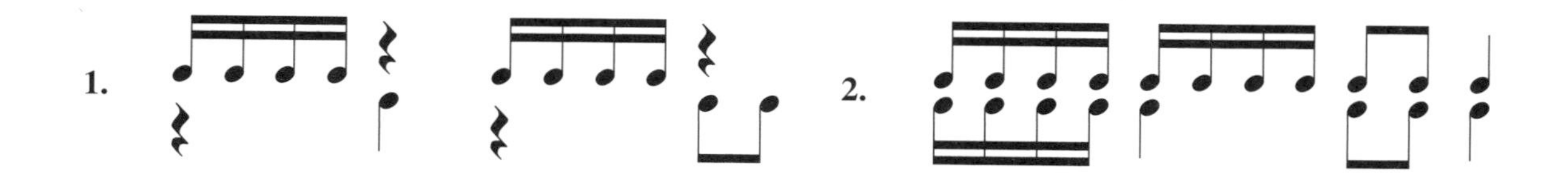

Sight reading—Plan the tonic and dominant chords first.

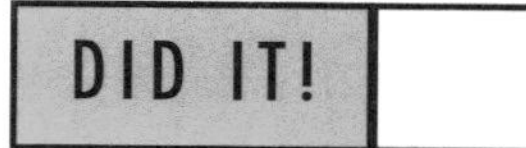

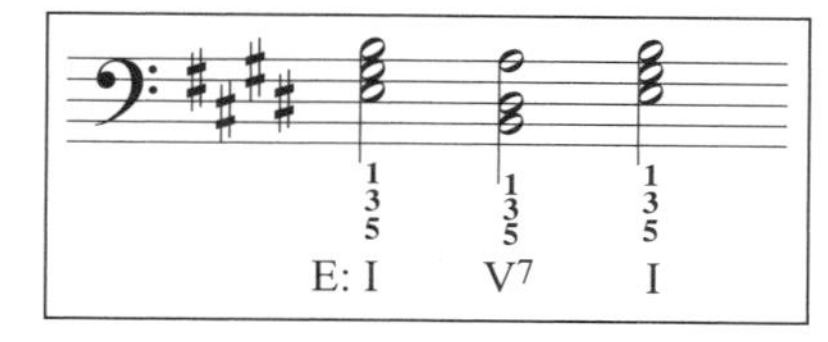

Tap the rhythm hands together. Then play the piece silently on the top of the keys before playing it with confidence until the end!

Transpose this piece to the keys of:

F major _____ D major _____

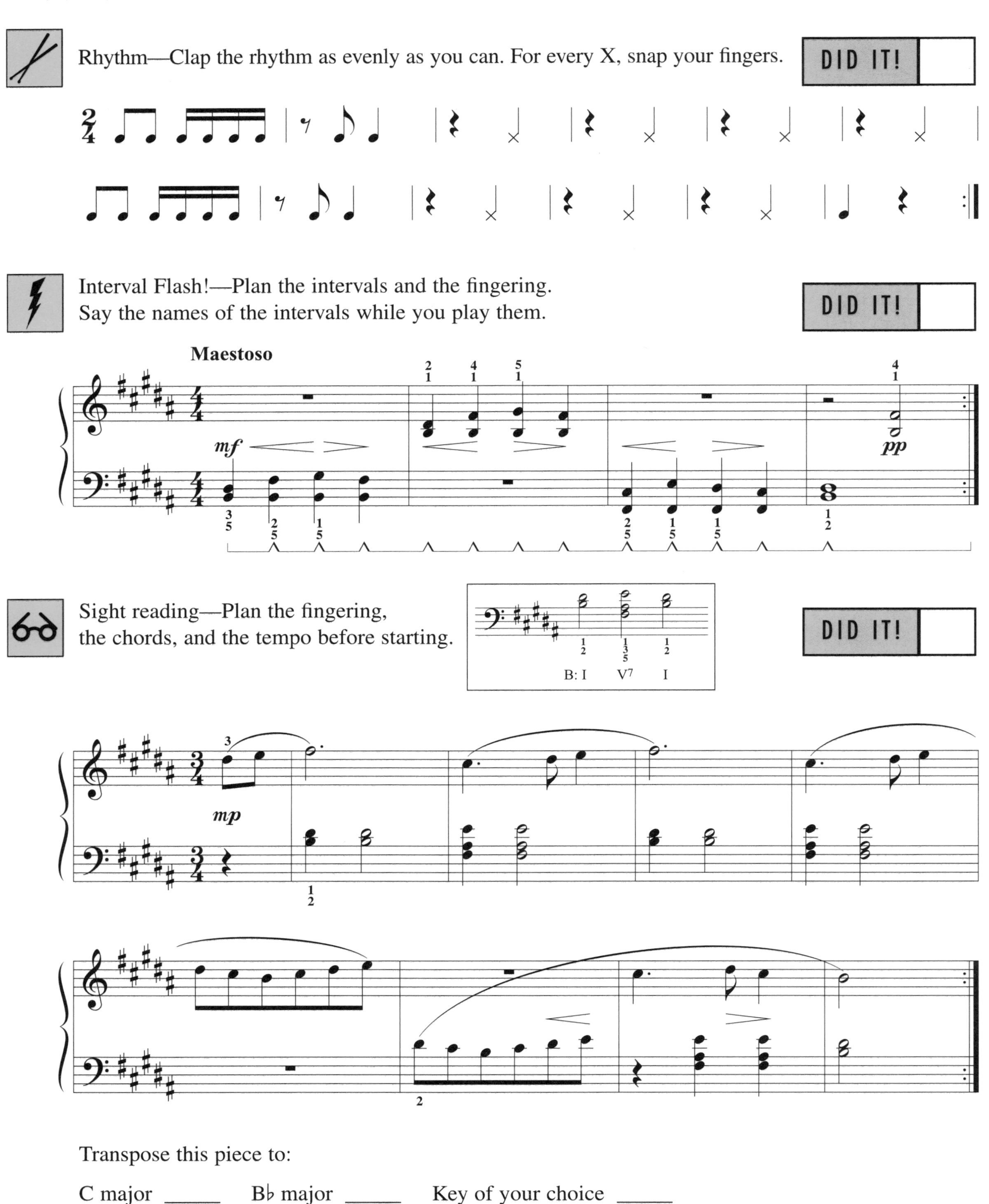

Rhythm—Clap the rhythm as evenly as you can. For every X, snap your fingers.

DID IT!

Interval Flash!—Plan the intervals and the fingering.
Say the names of the intervals while you play them.

DID IT!

Sight reading—Plan the fingering, the chords, and the tempo before starting.

DID IT!

Transpose this piece to:

C major _____ B♭ major _____ Key of your choice _____

Ensemble Piece

DID IT!

Your teacher will give you 2 minutes to prepare this piece silently.

Summer Sailboats

Teacher accompaniment (student plays one octave higher)

After playing, ask yourself, "Did I keep going no matter what happened?"

Unit 3

DAY ONE

New Concepts: sixteenth-note rhythms (♬♬) in the keys of B flat and E flat major; pieces with IV^6_4-I and V^6_5-I cadences

Rhythm—Clap the following with confidence, and *crescendo* to every downbeat.

DID IT!

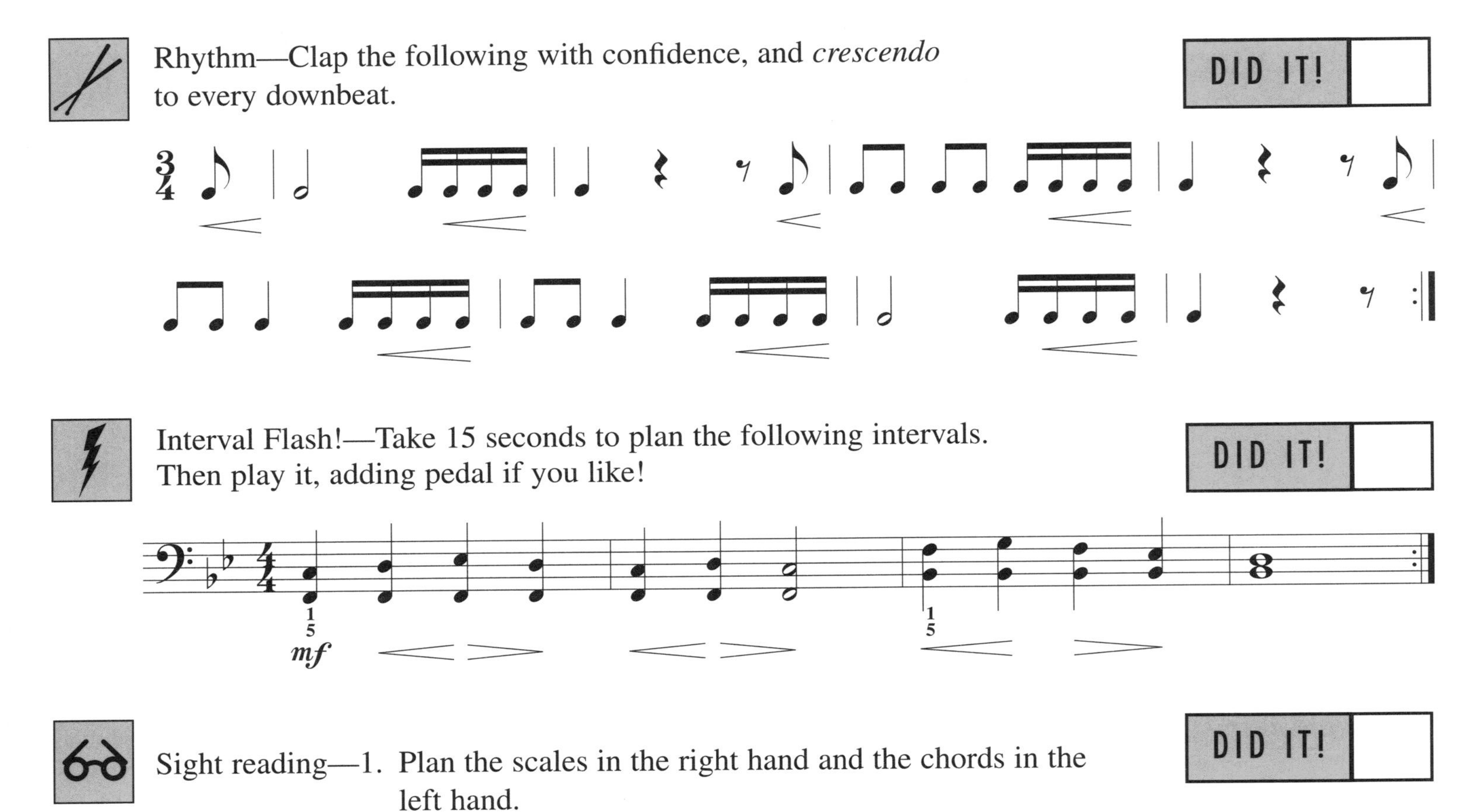

Interval Flash!—Take 15 seconds to plan the following intervals. Then play it, adding pedal if you like!

DID IT!

Sight reading—1. Plan the scales in the right hand and the chords in the left hand.

2. With the metronome at ♪=96, play from the beginning to the end without stopping.

Try playing the piece faster. How would you rate yourself?

flawless _____ decent _____ needs work _____

Transpose this piece to the following keys:

C major _____ F major _____

Rhythm—Say the following lyrics while pointing to each note.

DID IT!

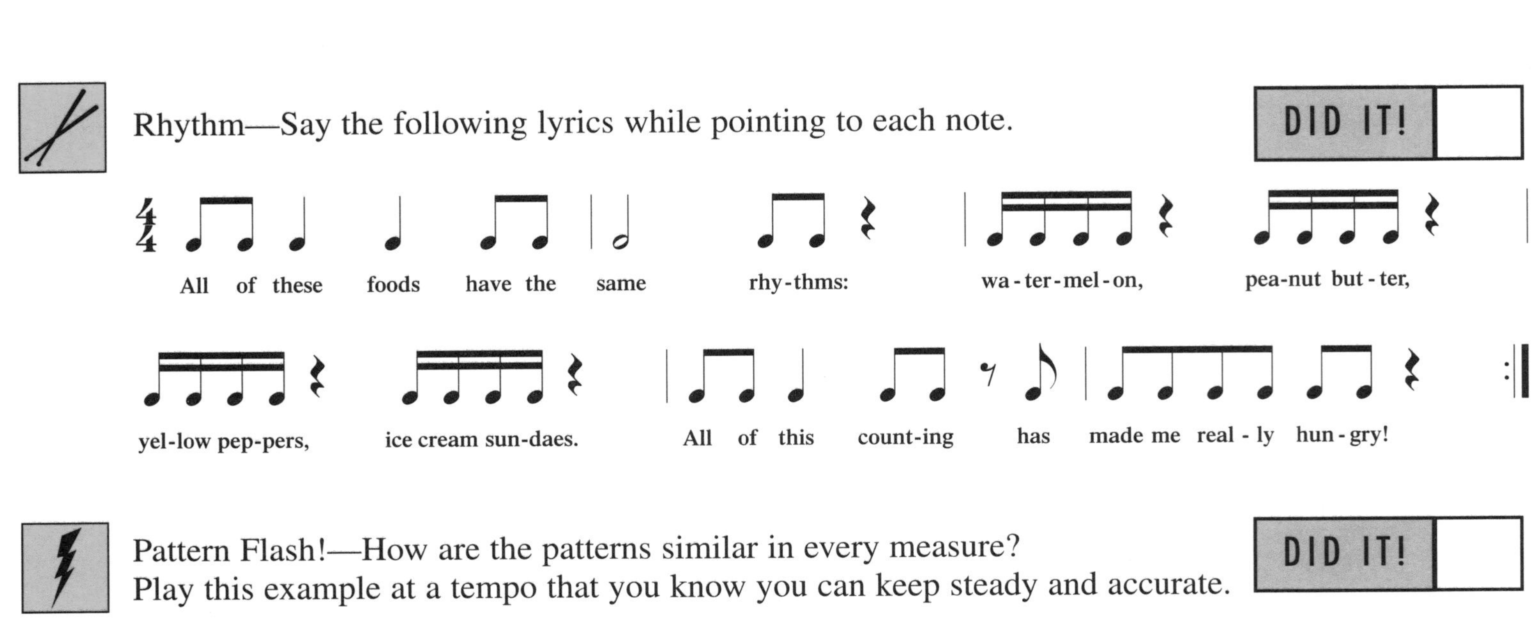

Pattern Flash!—How are the patterns similar in every measure?
Play this example at a tempo that you know you can keep steady and accurate.

DID IT!

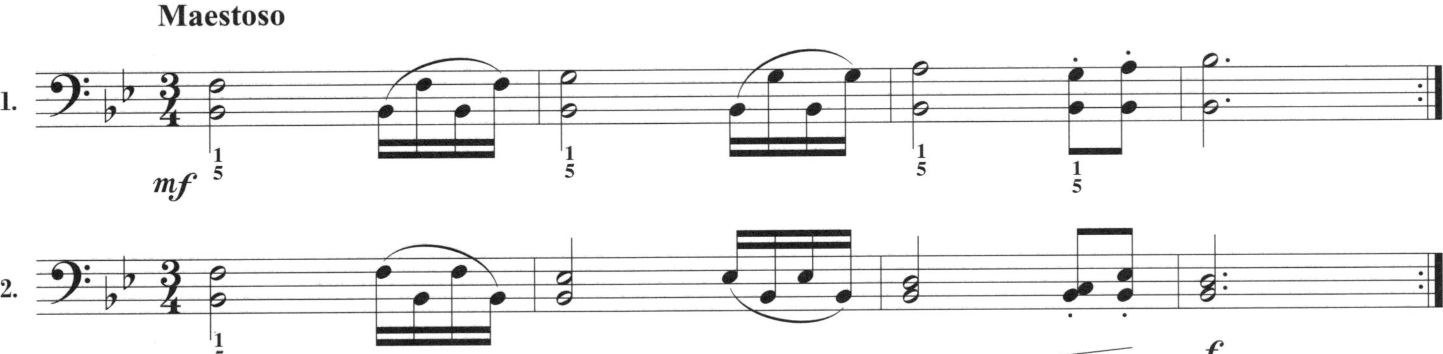

Sight reading—Play the tonic and dominant chords in the left hand first.

DID IT!

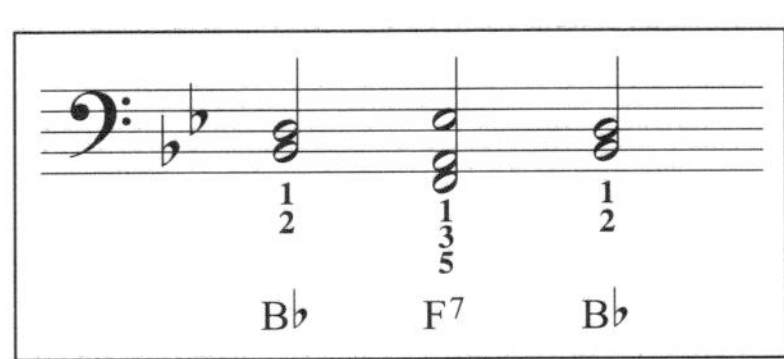

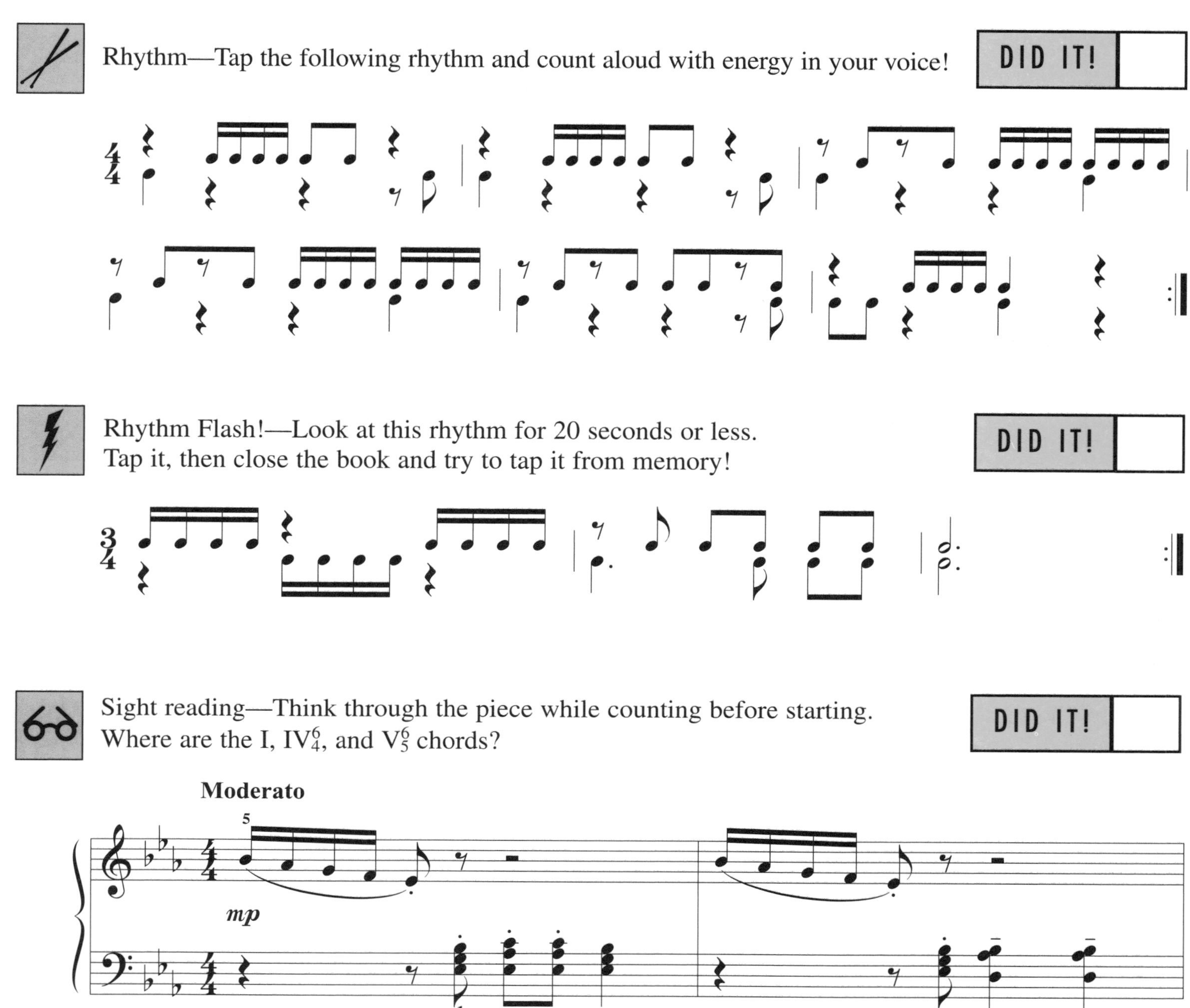

Rhythm—Tap the following rhythm and count aloud with energy in your voice!

DID IT!

Rhythm Flash!—Look at this rhythm for 20 seconds or less.
Tap it, then close the book and try to tap it from memory!

DID IT!

Sight reading—Think through the piece while counting before starting.
Where are the I, IV$^6_4$, and V$^6_5$ chords?

DID IT!

Rhythm—There are three mistakes below. Fix them and then clap and count with confidence!

DID IT!

Interval Flash!—How are the two interval flashes different? Once you plan these, play them!

DID IT!

Sight reading—Plan the left-hand chords. Block (playing the individual notes of the chords at the same time) the left hand while playing the right hand. Then play as written.

DID IT!

Key of _____

Transpose this piece to the keys of:

E major _____ D major _____ F major _____

Ensemble Piece

DID IT!

Before playing as written, block all of the intervals in the right hand. The circled notes show you how.

Stock Car Races

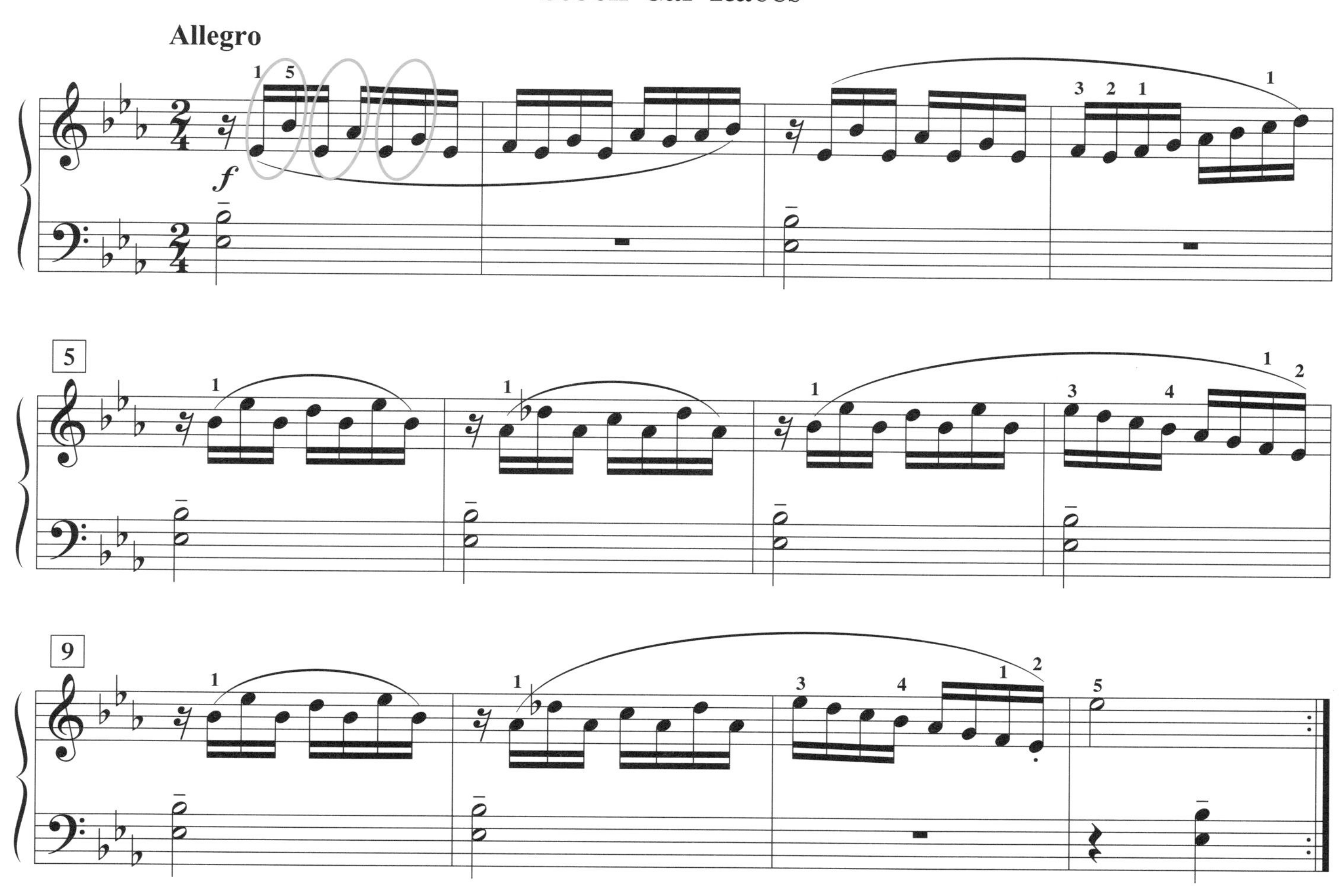

Teacher accompaniment (student plays as written)

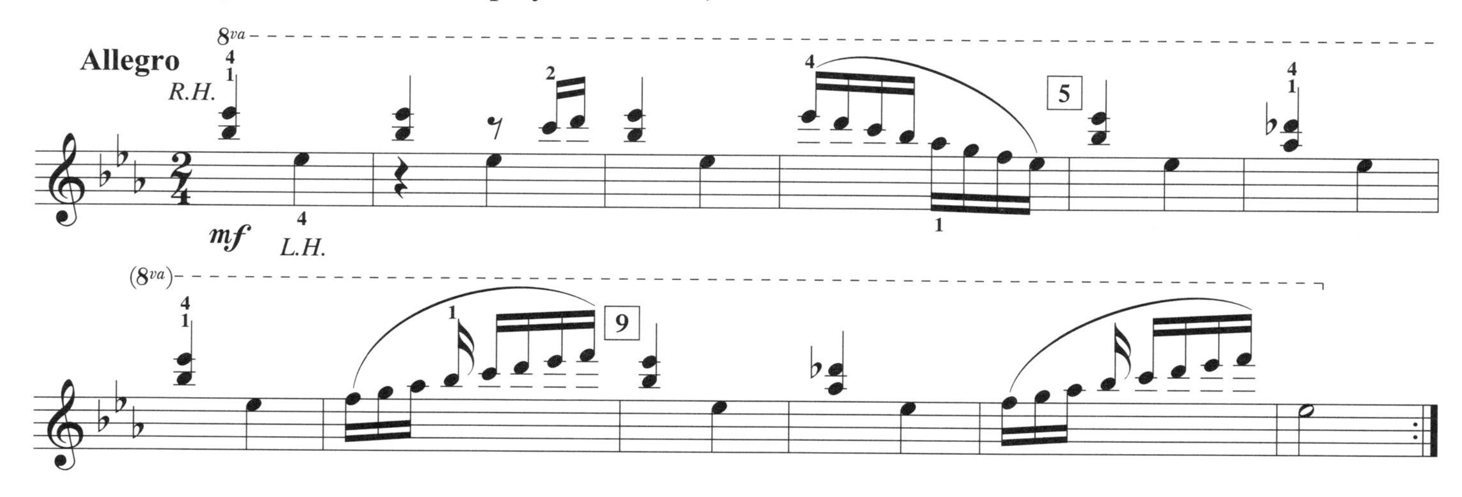

?

After playing, ask yourself, "Did I play the piece *f* and with confidence?"

Unit 4

New Concept: sixteenth-note rhythms (♪♬)

Rhythm—Circle all of the rhythms that look like this: ♪♬ 1 (e) + a
Then tap and count aloud.

DID IT!

Pattern Flash!—What is the recurring pattern in this piece?

DID IT!

Allegretto

Sight reading—Tap and count aloud for the following piece.
Plan each pattern, remembering the B flats!

DID IT!

Andante

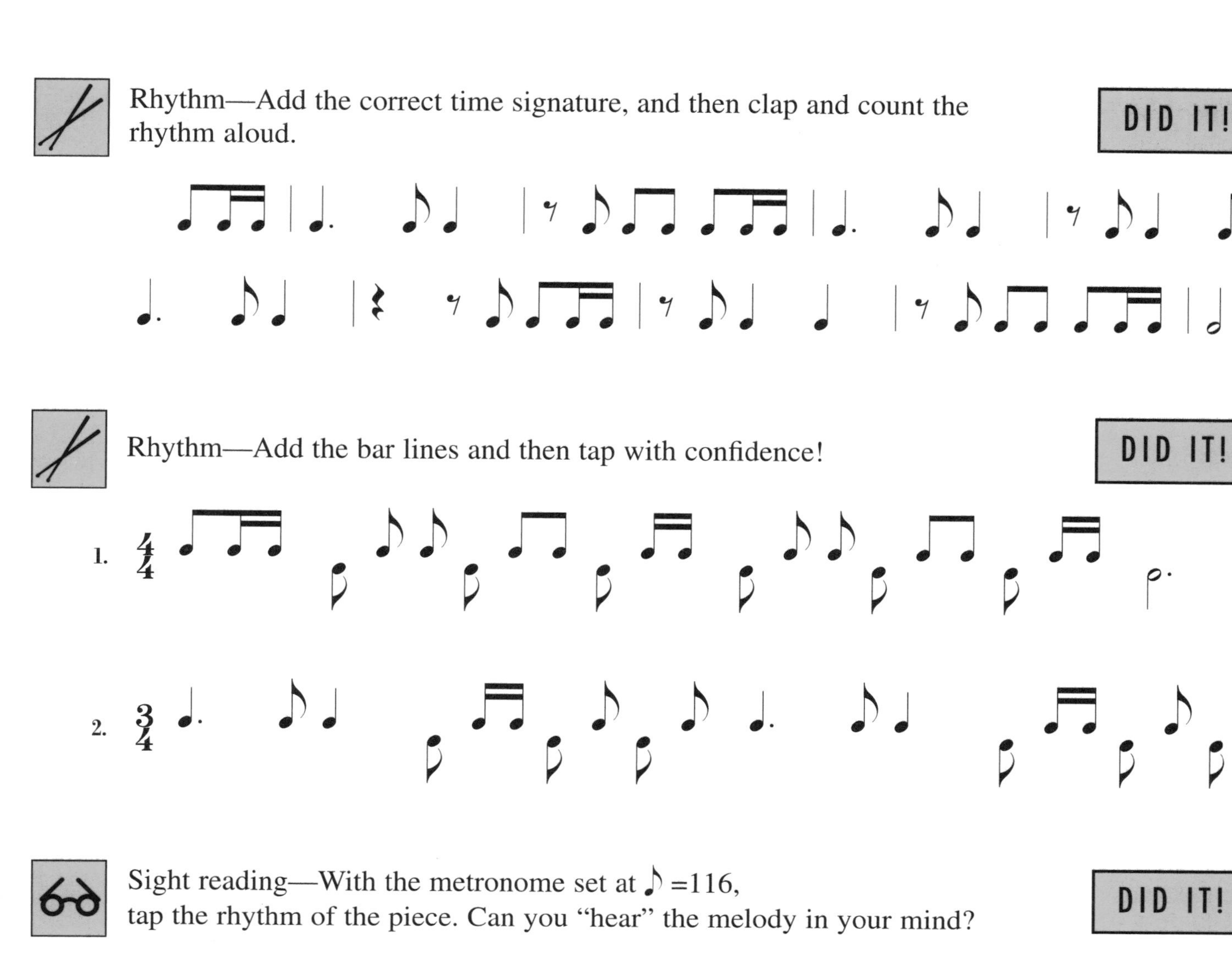

Rhythm—Add the correct time signature, and then clap and count the rhythm aloud.

DID IT!

Rhythm—Add the bar lines and then tap with confidence!

DID IT!

Sight reading—With the metronome set at ♪ =116, tap the rhythm of the piece. Can you "hear" the melody in your mind?

DID IT!

Rhythm—Fill in the empty measures with notes or rests. Choose one metronome marking to tap the rhythm evenly: ♪ = 96 or ♪ = 112.

DID IT!

Interval Flash!—Which two intervals are incorrect? Correct them and then play the exercise.

DID IT!

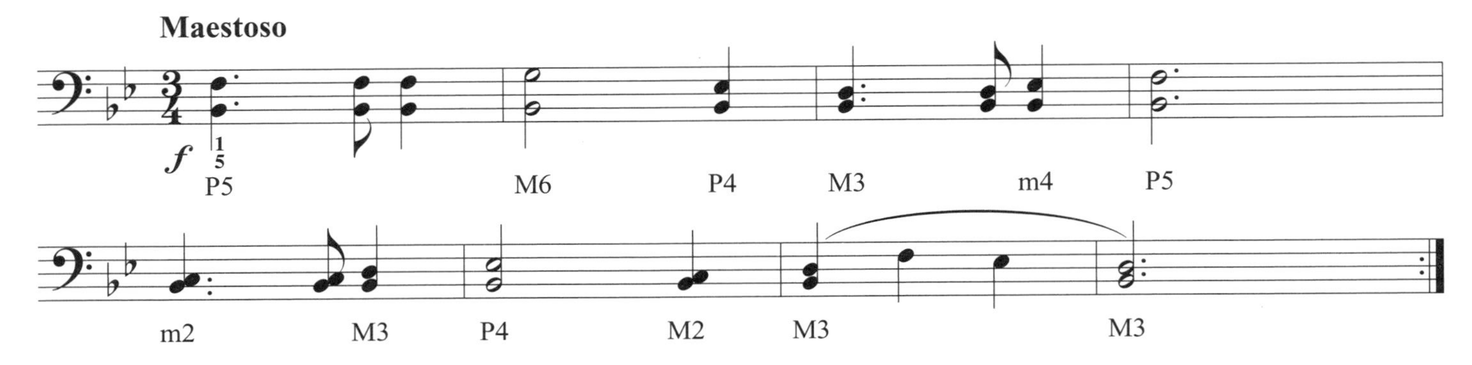

Sight reading—Give yourself the opening pitch in the right hand.
Can you sing the melody aloud? What are the slurred intervals in the left hand?
3rds 4ths 5ths 6ths (circle the answer/s). Set an ♪ pulse before you begin.

DID IT!

If you sight read without stopping, place a smiley face on the line: _____

Rhythm—Clap and count with energy in your voice!

DID IT!

Rhythm Flash!—Look at the first example for 10 seconds. Close the book and try to remember it! Then do the same for the second example.

DID IT!

Sight reading—With the metronome at ♩=96, tap the rhythm before playing. Plan the move up the octave before you begin.

DID IT!

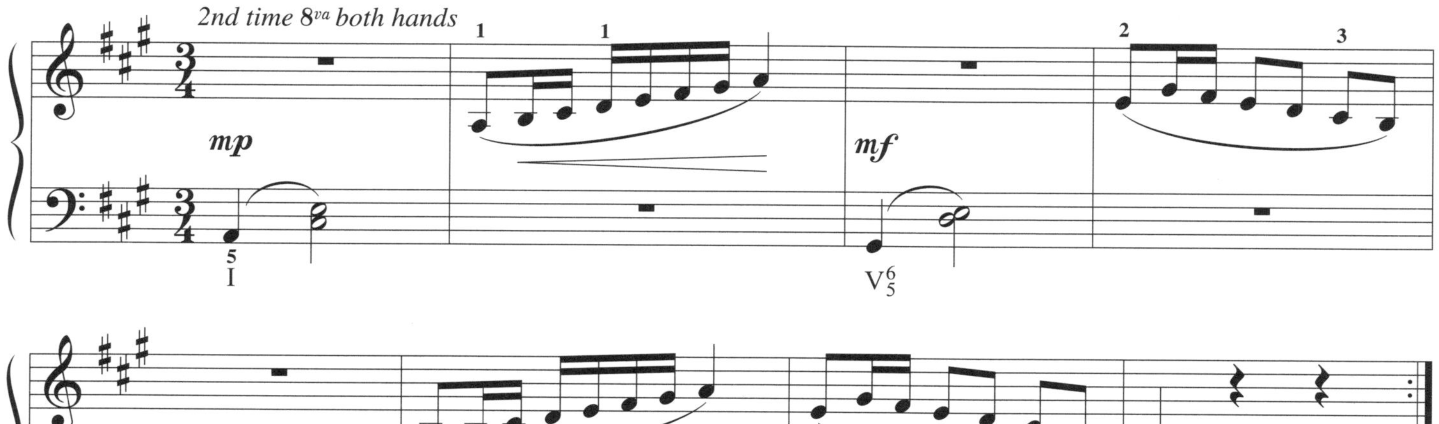

Rhythm—Tap the following rhythm with consistency and evenness.

DID IT!

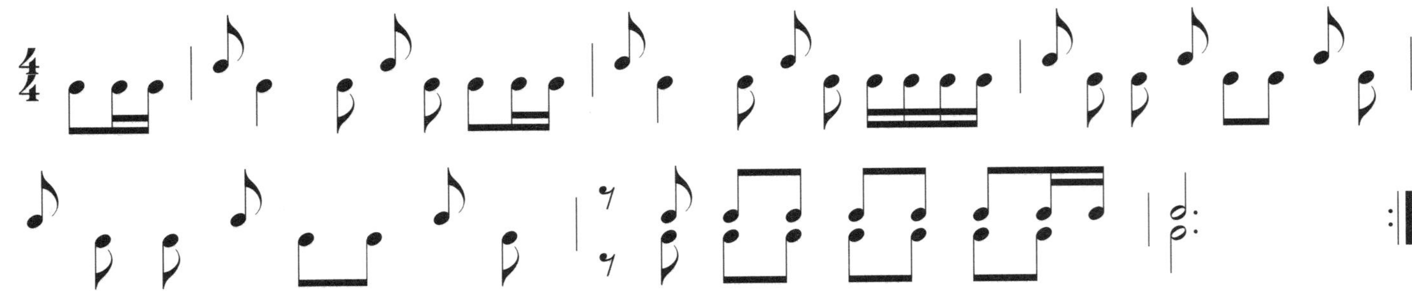

Pattern Flash!—How are the first two measures similar? Give yourself one chance to play them correctly, so plan it well before you start.

DID IT!

Sight reading—Can you play this piece without any fingerings marked in? Plan it before you begin.

DID IT!

Ensemble Piece

DID IT!

Before playing, plan the time and key signatures, and the rhythm.

Railroad Blues

Teacher accompaniment (student plays as written)

? After playing, ask yourself, "Did I play with a relaxed and free spirit?"

Unit 5

DAY ONE

New Concepts: sixteenth-note rhythms (♪ ♬) in the keys of A and D minor; pieces with i-iv$^6_4$-i-V$^6_5$-i cadences

Rhythm—Tap this rhythm:
Then tap the following while counting aloud.

DID IT!

Interval Flash!—Play the example. Then close the book and try to play it again!

DID IT!

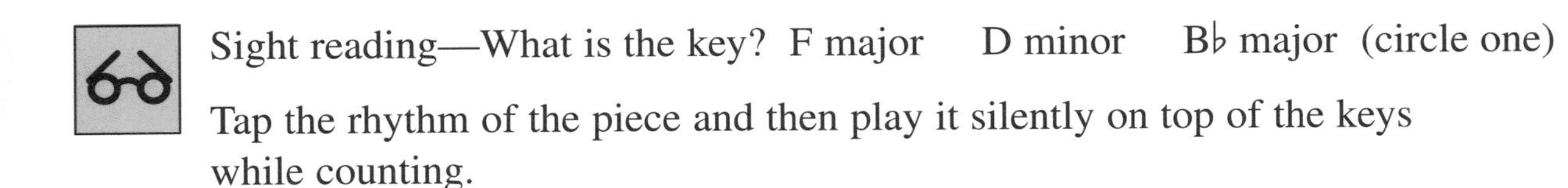

How successful were you? Very _____ OK _____

Sight reading—What is the key? F major D minor B♭ major (circle one)

DID IT!

Tap the rhythm of the piece and then play it silently on top of the keys while counting.

How would you rate your sight reading? super good so-so poor (circle one)

Can you play this piece with the metronome at ♪=108? _____

Rhythm—How quickly and accurately can you tap this rhythm hands together?

DID IT!

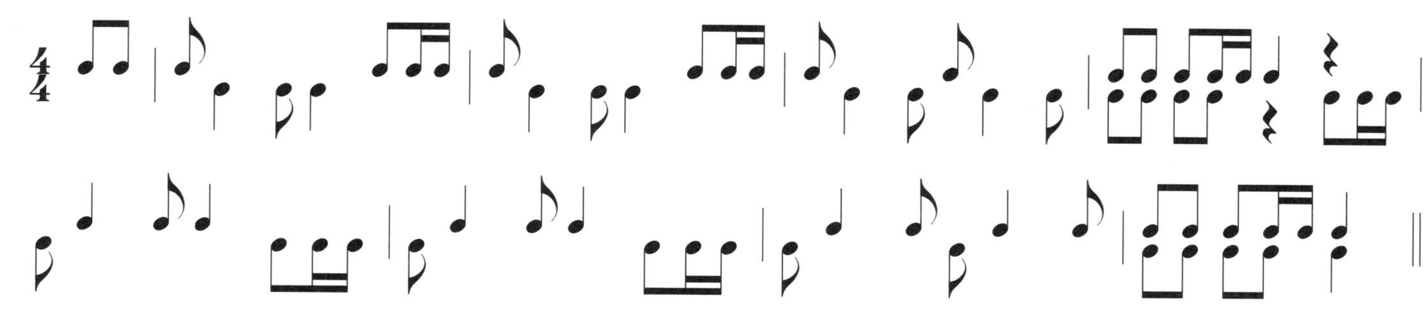

Rhythm Flash!—Take one minute or less to plan this rhythm flash.
Then try playing it without looking at the music!

DID IT!

Now try it in G minor _____ F minor _____

Sight reading—Play the cadence first.

DID IT!

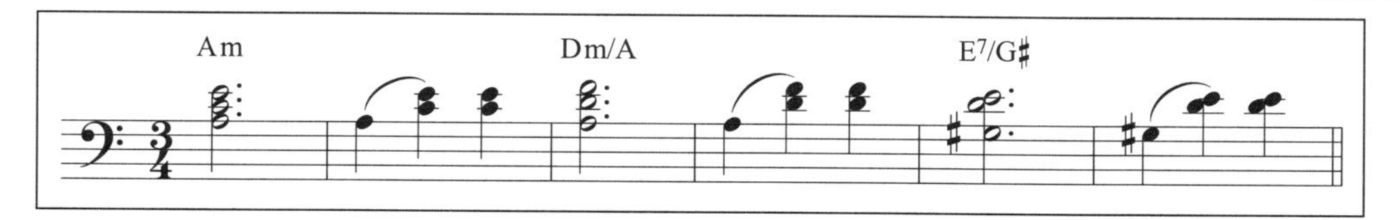

Then prepare the four phrases in the right hand. You are ready to begin! Choose to play either blocked chords or a waltz bass in your left hand.

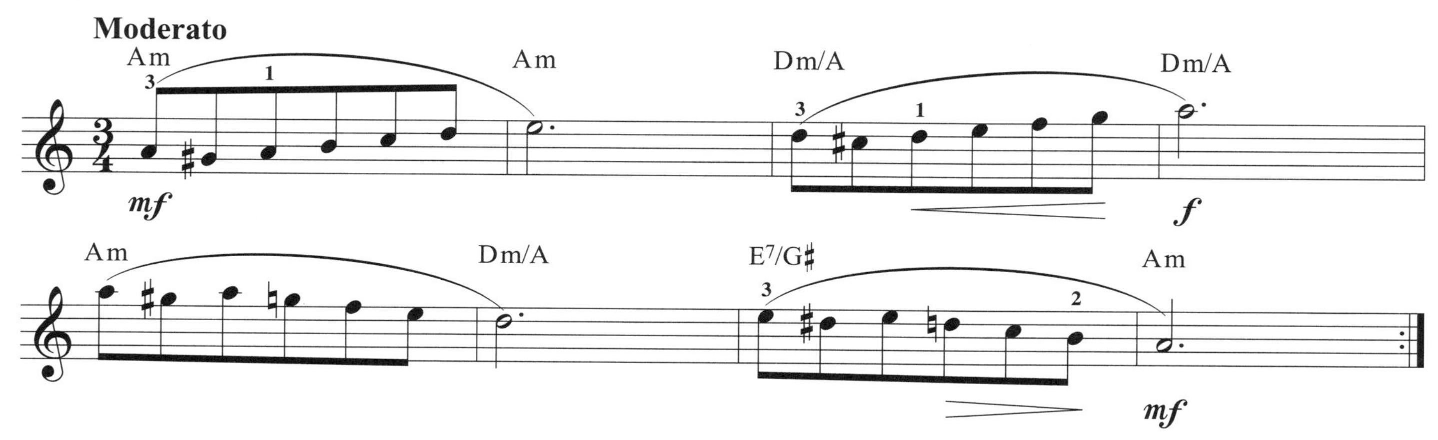

Rhythm—Using this rhythm, improvise a melody with your left hand in the key of D minor. The D minor scale is D E F G A B♭ C♯ D.

DID IT!

Is this natural, harmonic, or melodic minor? (circle one)

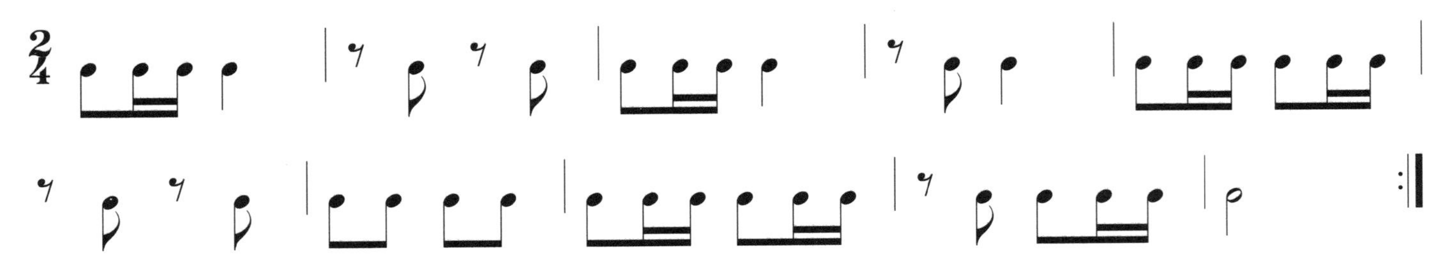

Interval Flash!—How are the first two measures alike? Add your own fingering and count while you play.

DID IT!

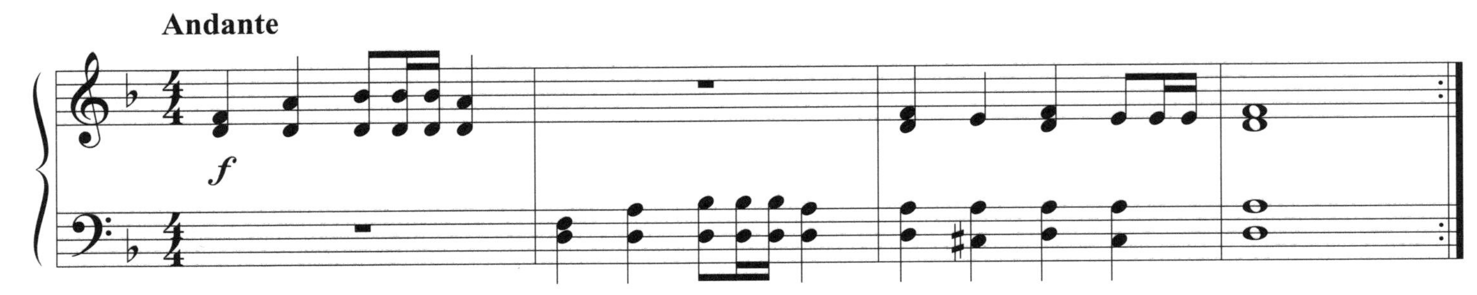

Sight reading—Be sure to check the time signature before playing. Plan the patterns under your fingers.

DID IT!

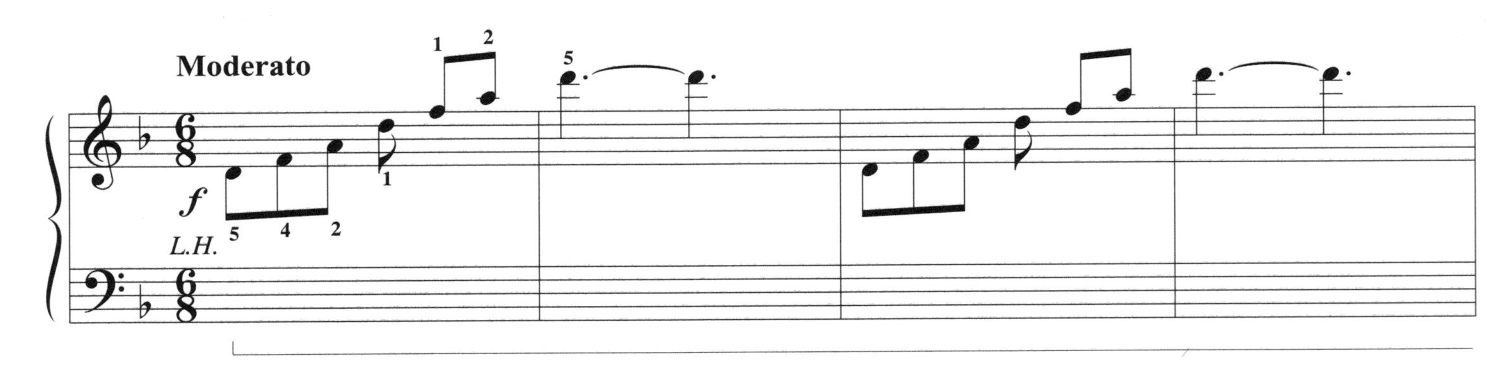

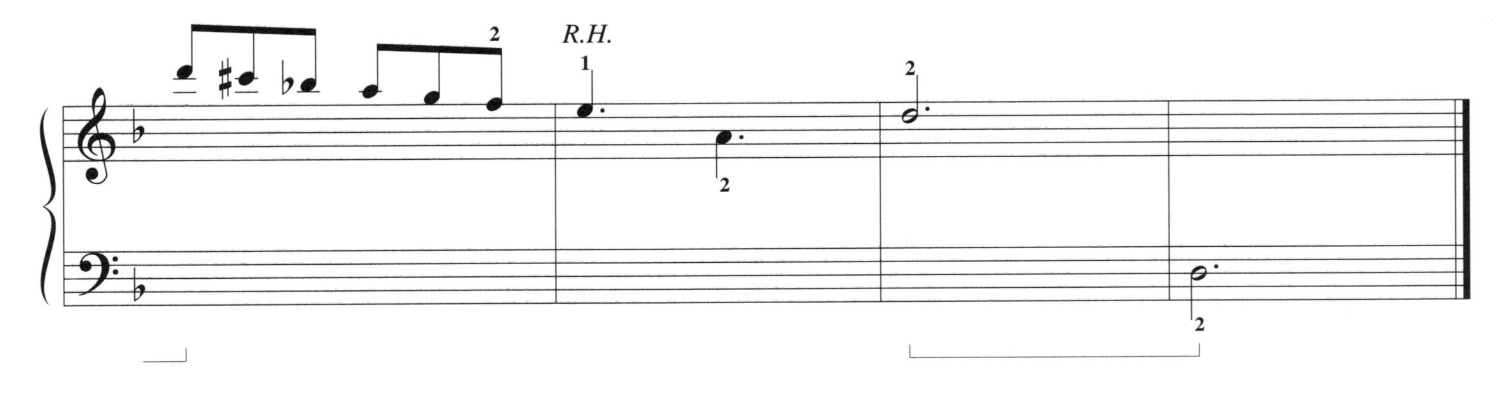

Rhythm—With the metronome set at ♩. = 72, tap the rhythm.

DID IT!

Pattern Flash!—Take ten seconds or less to play the first pattern flash. Then try the next one.

DID IT!

Sight reading—Prepare the chords in the right hand. Then tap the rhythm hands together. Plan a tempo that you can keep steady.

DID IT!

Rhythm—Clap the rhythm evenly and accurately.

DID IT!

Pattern Flash!—Look at the example and plan it for 40 seconds or less. Choose your own fingering. Then close the book and play it!

DID IT!

Sight reading—Plan the left hand jumps first.

DID IT!

Ensemble Piece

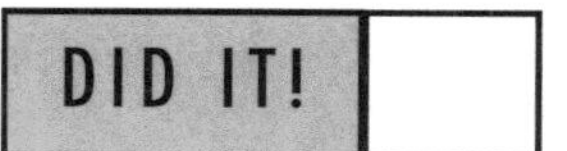

Add the fingering if you need to before playing. Plan the rhythm and the chords.

Old Silent Movies

Teacher accompaniment (student plays one octave higher)

? After playing, ask yourself, "Did I play the articulations as well as I could?"

Unit 6

New Concept: sixteenth-note rhythms (♩. ♬)

Rhythm—Tap this rhythm: 1 (e +) a 2 (e +) a 3

Then tap the following while counting aloud.

Rhythm Flash!—Look at example 1 for 10 seconds or less. Close the book and try to remember it exactly! Then try the same with example 2.

Sight reading—With the metronome set at ♪=112, clap the rhythm of the right-hand melody until secure. Count while you play and remember to subdivide the beats!

DID IT!

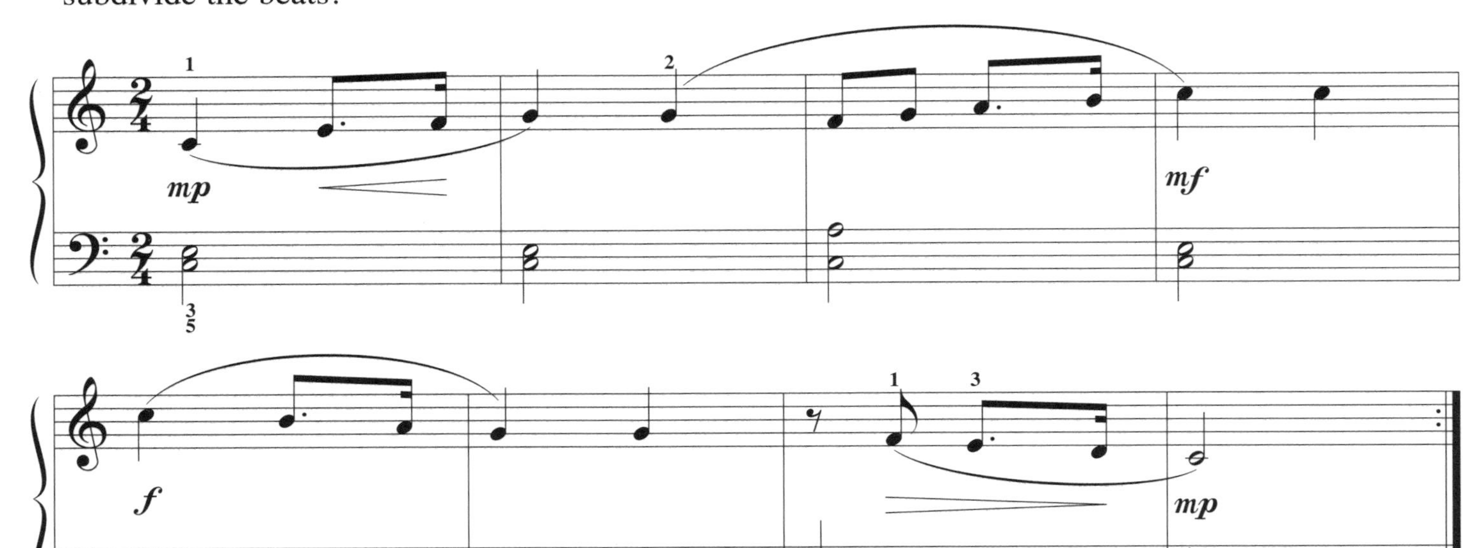

Transpose this piece to the keys of:

D major _____ E major _____ G major _____

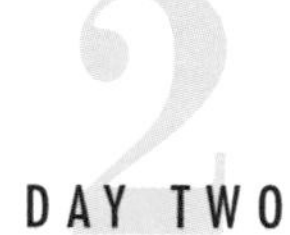

Rhythm—Tap a steady eighth-note pulse and speak these words:

DID IT!

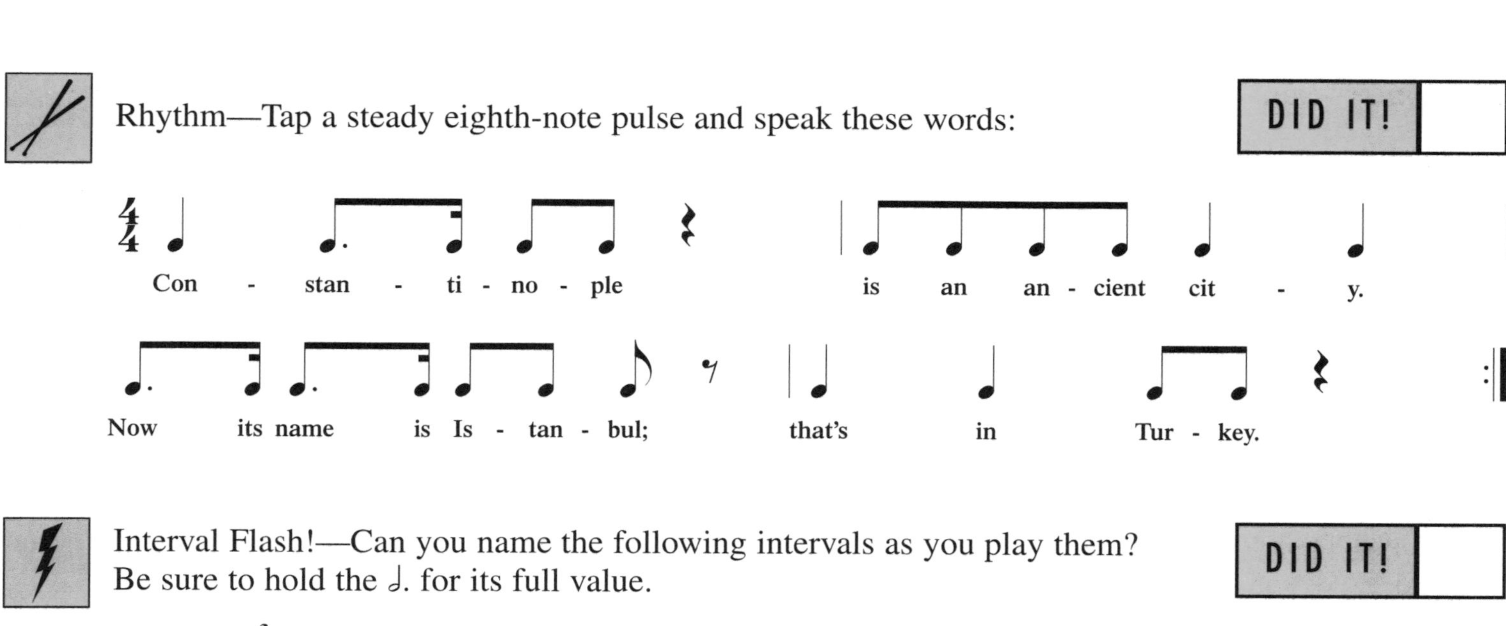

Interval Flash!—Can you name the following intervals as you play them?
Be sure to hold the 𝅗𝅥. for its full value.

DID IT!

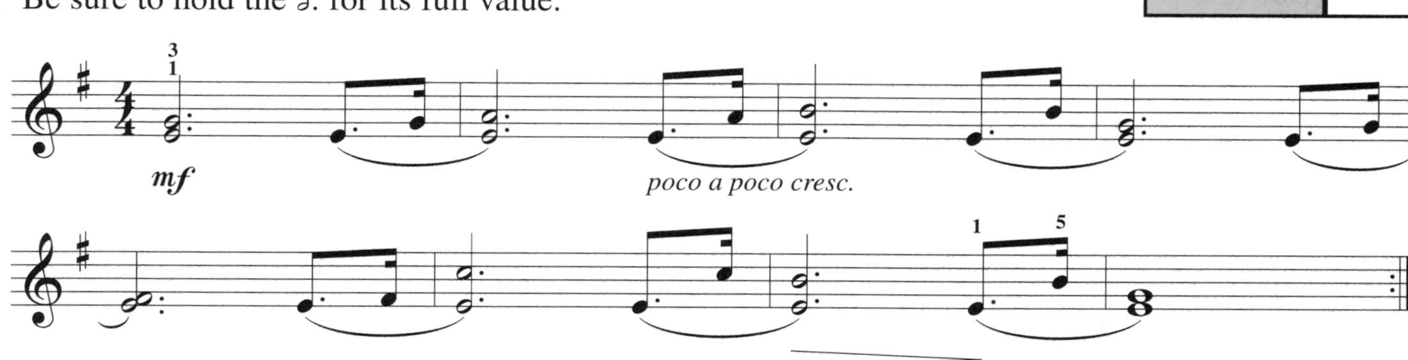

Sight reading—How are these two examples similar? How are they different?
With the metronome set to ♩=108, tap the rhythm of both hands together.
Listen carefully to the steadiness of the dotted rhythms.

DID IT!

Rhythm—When you see a note with an "X," snap your fingers. Count and clap this rhythm with complete steadiness.

DID IT!

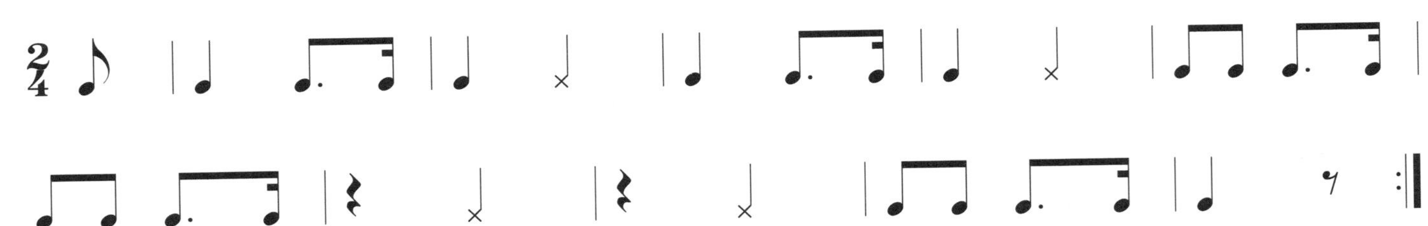

Sight reading—Plan the i, iv^6_4, and V^6_5 chords in the left hand. Then use the waltz pattern in the left hand while playing the right-hand melody. Add the dynamics too!

DID IT!

How is this harmonization similar/different than the previous piece?

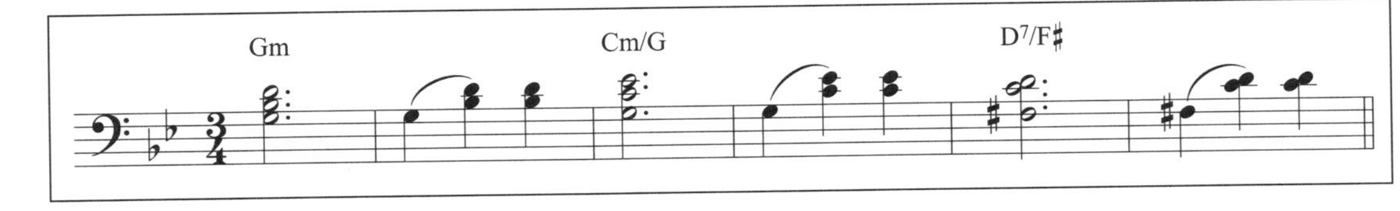

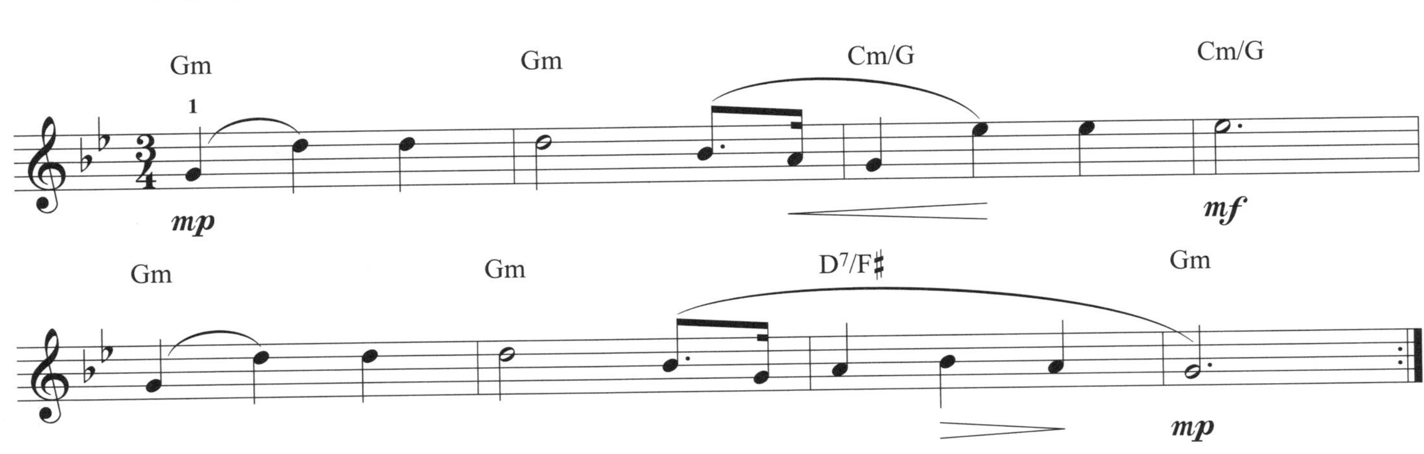

Rhythm—Add bar lines to the following examples, and then tap and count aloud.

Pattern Flash!—Play the first example, being sure to subdivide the dotted rhythms. Can you play it again, from memory? Then do the same with the second example.

Sight reading—Tap the rhythm hands together. Before beginning, choose a tempo that you can keep steady.

Transpose this piece to the keys of:

G minor _____ E minor _____

Rhythm—With the metronome set at ♪=132, tap the following:
DID IT!
Rhythm—Use the metronome at ♩=96 in order to help you with this rhythm.
DID IT!
Dot - ted eighth, six-teenth, dot - ted eighth, six-teenth, when you count or sing and you
want to make it swing, use dot - ted eighth, six-teenth, dot - ted eighth, six-teenth!
Sight reading—Tap the rhythm first. Plan the key. Play without looking at your hands.
DID IT!
Andante
mf legato
L.H. over
p

Ensemble Piece

DID IT!

Plan the left-hand fingering first. Can you "sing" the melody in your head before you play the piece?

A Sad, Sad, Sad, Sad Song

Teacher accompaniment (student plays one octave higher)

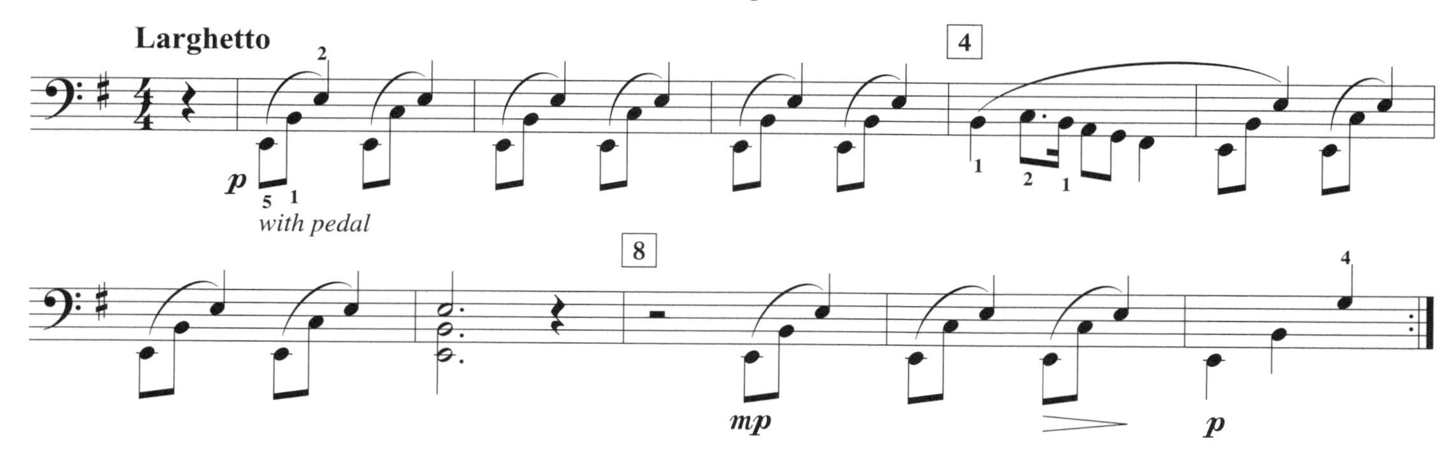

After playing, ask yourself, "Did I play with feeling?"

Unit 7

1
DAY ONE

New Concepts: pieces in the keys of B flat, E flat, A flat, and D flat major; music term: *senza*

Rhythm—Crescendo to each downbeat as you clap and count.

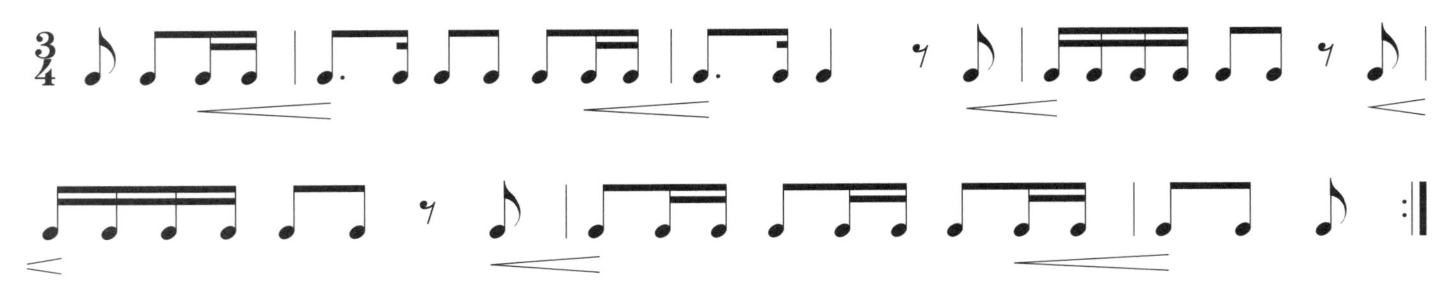

Rhythm Flash!—Count this rhythm in your head. When you think you can do it from memory, close the book and try it again!

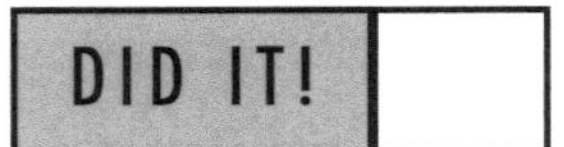

Sight reading—Notice the similar rhythmic patterns in both hands. Then tap it hands together. Silently play the piece on the top of the keys before playing at a steady tempo.

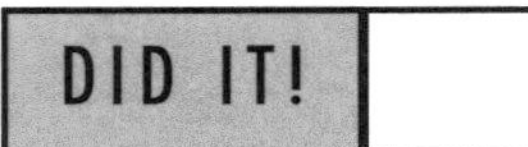

Key of _____

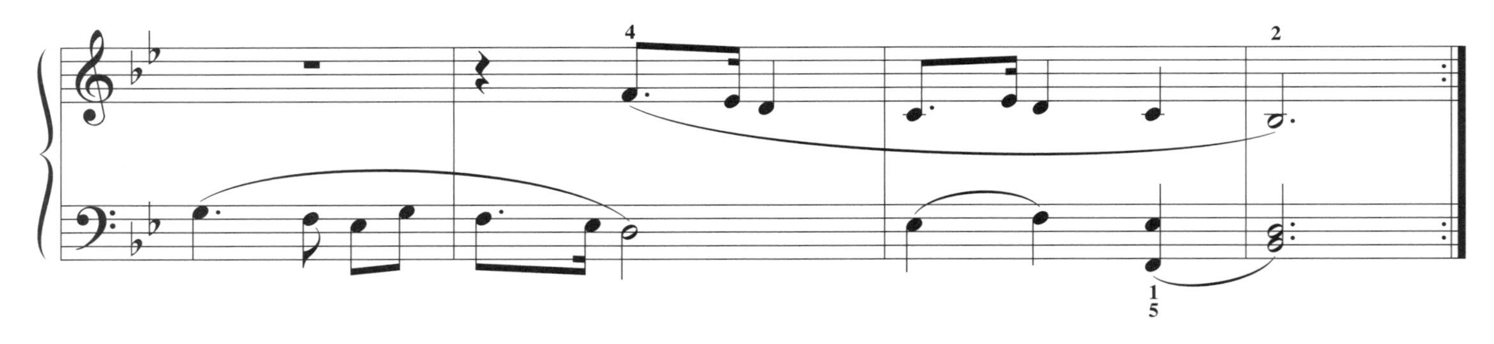

Transpose this piece to the keys of:

C major _____ B major _____

Rhythm—Add notes and rests in the blank measures. In the key of B♭ major, improvise a melody using the following rhythm. Be sure to count while you play.

DID IT!

Sight reading—Silently play this example first. Decide your own dynamics.

DID IT!

Sight reading—Once you begin this piece, don't stop until the very end.

DID IT!

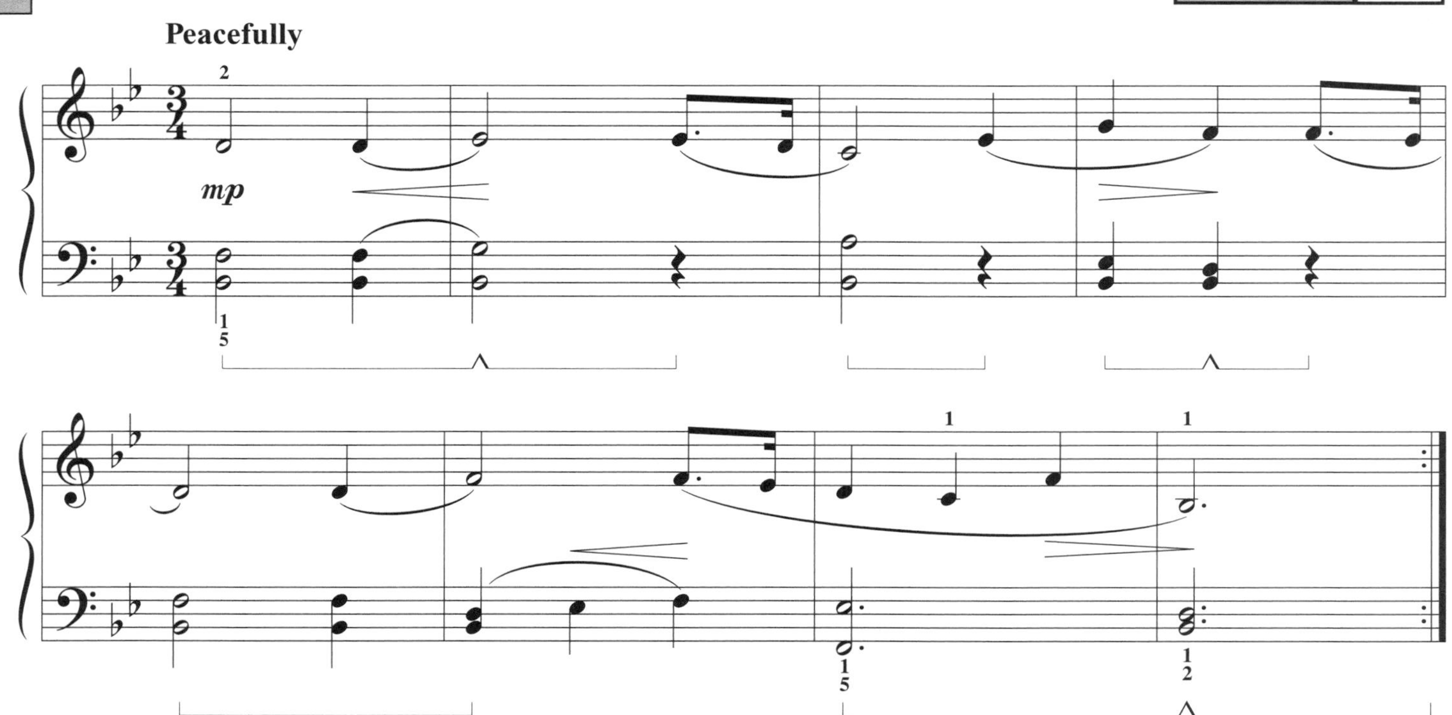

Transpose this piece to C major.

Rhythm—With the metronome at ♪=108, point to each note and speak the lyrics with energy!

DID IT!

Rhythm Flash!—Tap and count each example. Plan a tempo you can keep steady.

DID IT!

1. 4 (e +) a 1 + 2 + 3 + 4 (e +) a 1 + 2 + 3 +

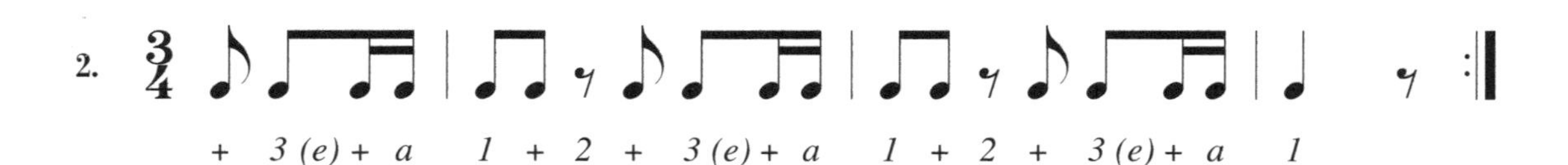

Sight reading—Plan the right-hand fingering. Play the piece silently on top of the keys while counting aloud. Look at the music and not your hands!

DID IT!

Transpose this piece to the keys of:

D major _____ E major _____ Key of your choice _____

Rhythm—Tap this rhythm on the fallboard of the piano evenly!

DID IT!

Pattern Flash!—Plan the fingering for the first example. Once you play it, can you play it back from memory? Then try the same with the second example.

DID IT!

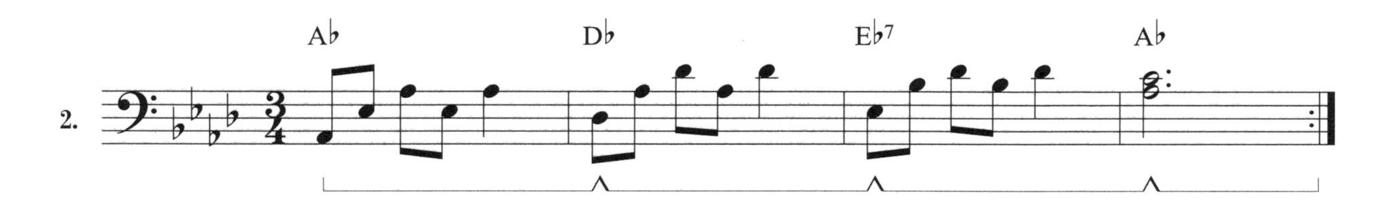

Sight reading—Does the right hand play outside of the A♭ major five-finger pattern? Play this example using blocked or broken chords in the left hand. (Use the left-hand patterns below for the lead sheet.)

DID IT!

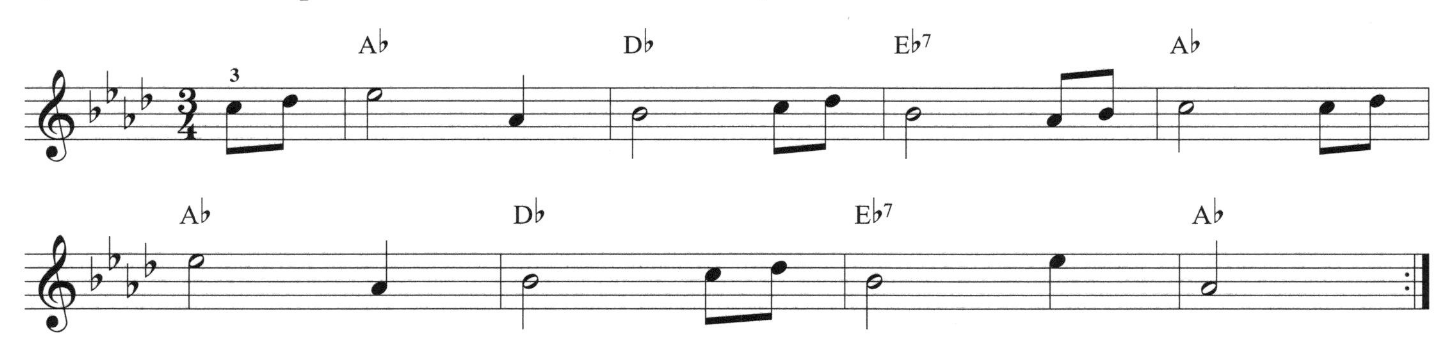

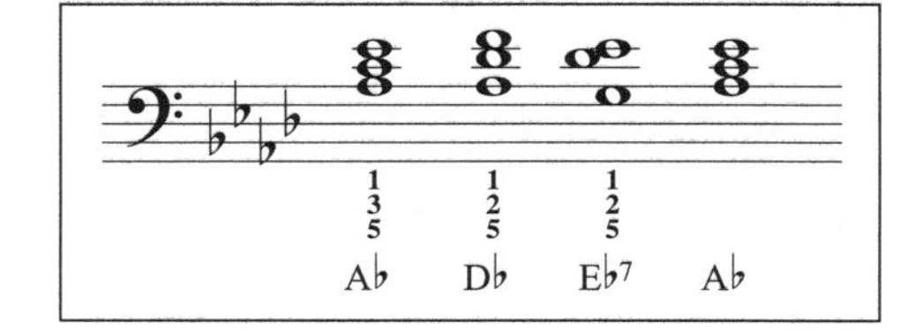

Rhythm—Clap and count with energy!

DID IT!

Rhythm—Plan the key, fingering, and tempo before beginning. Look at the music, not at your hands.

DID IT!

Sight reading—Tap and count the rhythm before playing.

DID IT!

Ensemble Piece

DID IT!

Before playing, plan the time and key signatures, and the rhythm.

Only Black Keys Allowed

Teacher accompaniment (student plays as written)

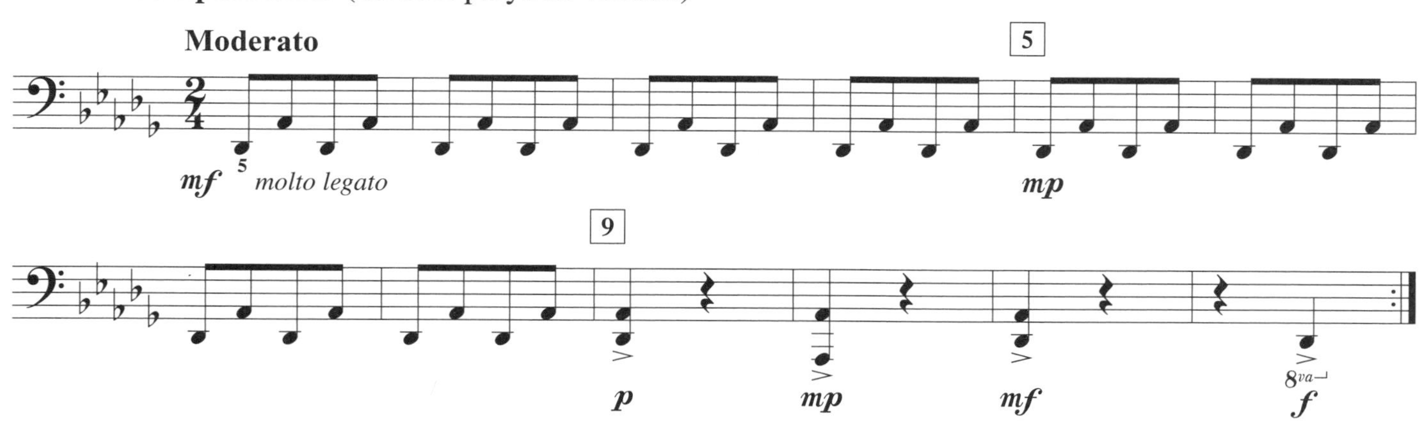

After playing, ask yourself, "Did I play the majority of the notes correctly?"

Unit 8

DAY ONE

New Concept: diminished triads in the keys of G and D

Rhythm—Add the bar lines, and then tap and count with energy!

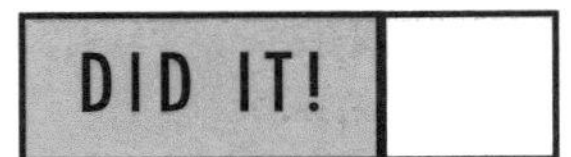

Chord Flash!—How accurately and quickly can you play the following chords?

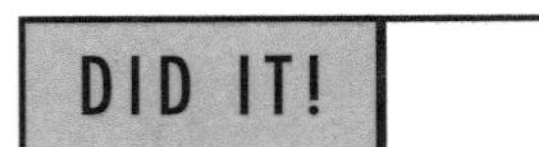

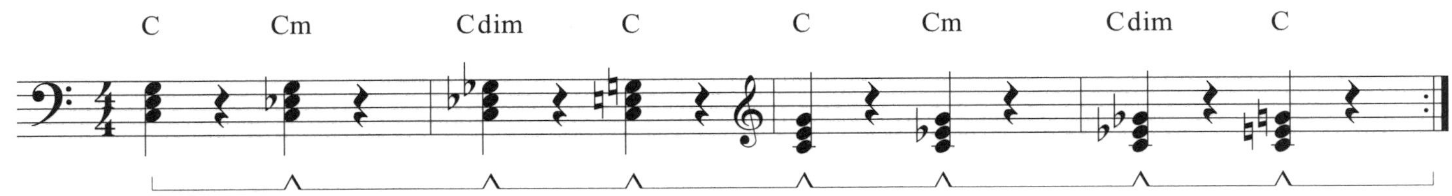

Sight reading—Play the opening pitch in the right hand. Can you "sing" the melody in your head? Circle all of the diminished chords before playing.

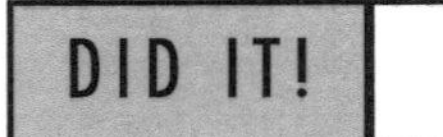

Transpose this piece to the keys of:

G major _____ D major _____ F major _____

Rhythm—Find the two mistakes below. Fix them, and then clap and count the rhythm aloud.

DID IT!

Sight reading—Plan the left-hand fingering. Silently play the piece on the top of the keys. Be sure to count and always look ahead!

DID IT!

Transpose this piece to the keys of:

A major _____ D major _____ F major _____

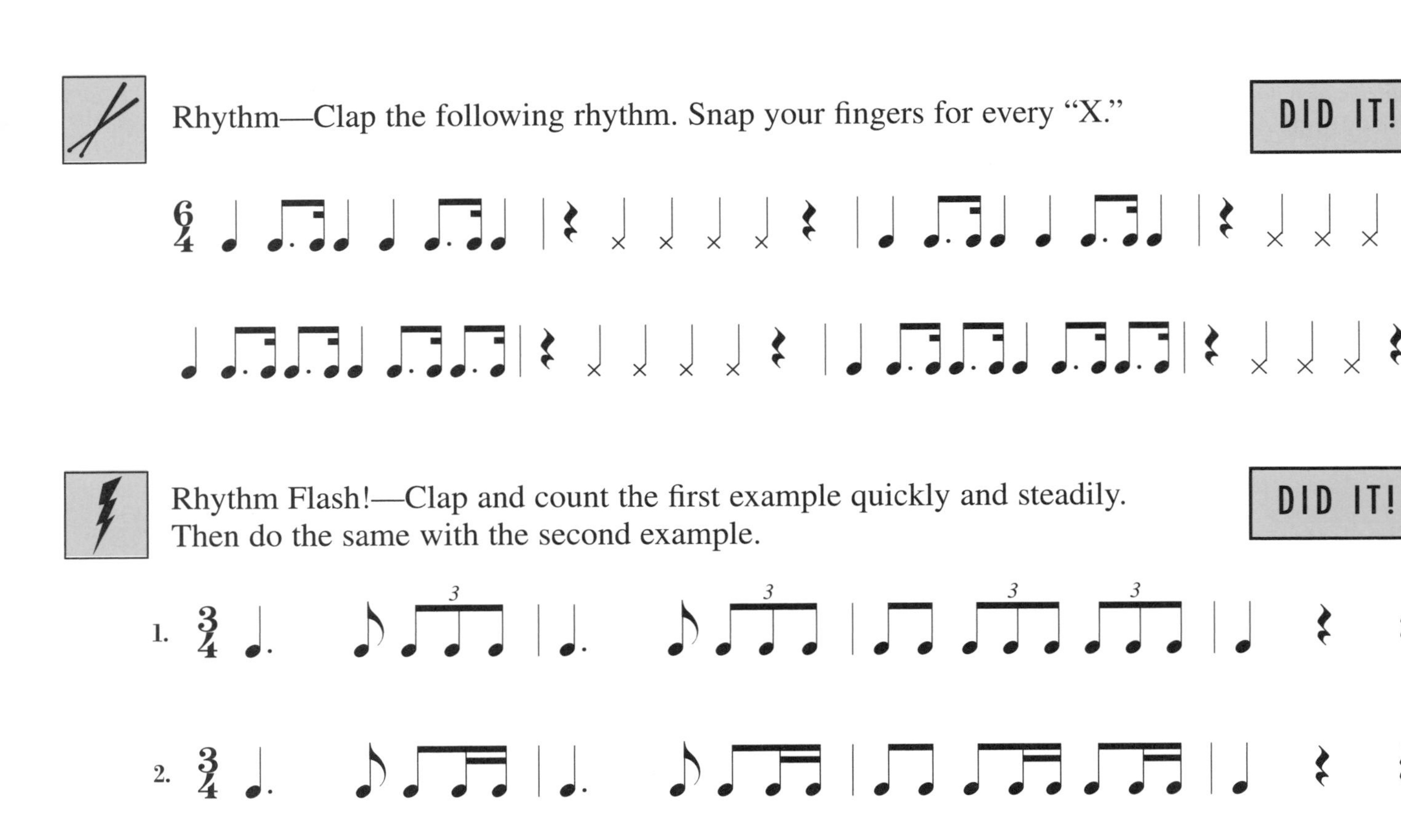

Rhythm—Clap the following rhythm. Snap your fingers for every "X."

DID IT!

Rhythm Flash!—Clap and count the first example quickly and steadily. Then do the same with the second example.

DID IT!

Sight reading—Plan the left-hand chords in order to complete this harmonization.

DID IT!

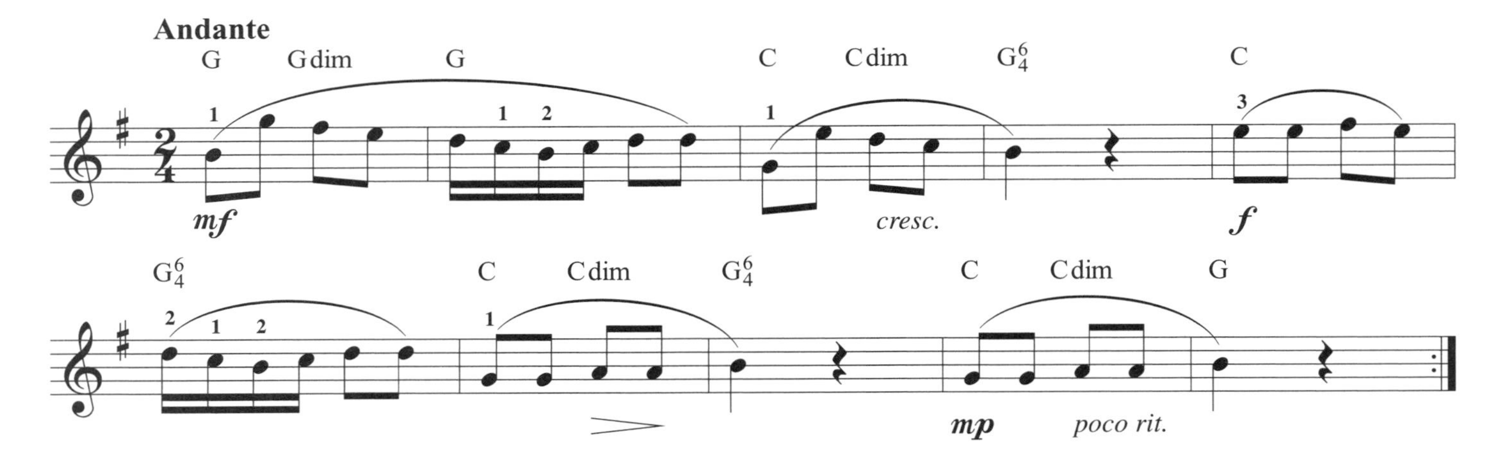

Rhythm—Set the metronome to a desired tempo. Tap and count with confidence!

DID IT!

Pattern Flash!—What is different between the 2 examples? Circle the diminished chords before you play.

DID IT!

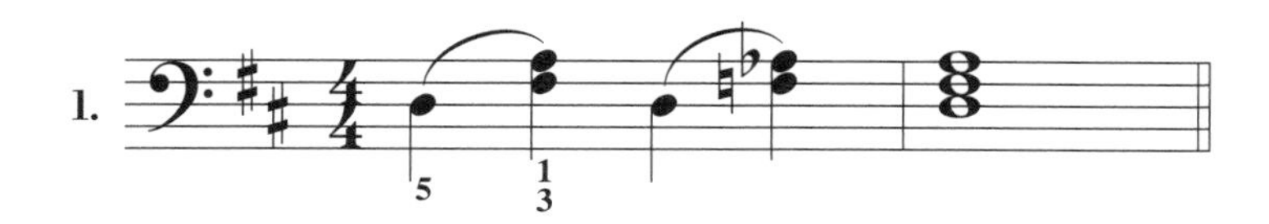

Sight reading—Plan the chords in the left hand before blocking them.

DID IT!

Rhythm—Tap the following with the metronome at ♩=76. It will be easier when you count aloud!

DID IT!

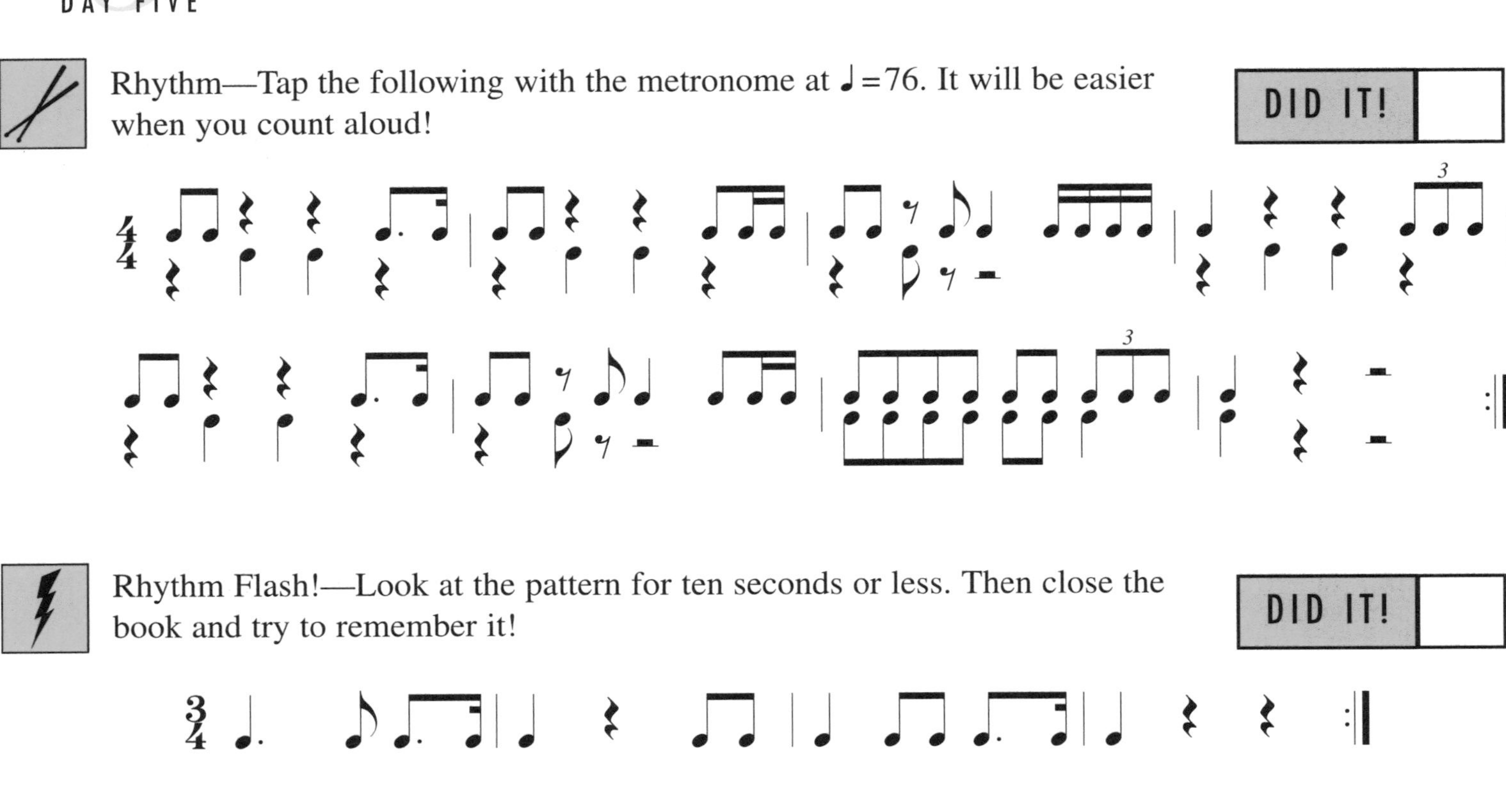

Rhythm Flash!—Look at the pattern for ten seconds or less. Then close the book and try to remember it!

DID IT!

Sight reading—Silently plan the left hand. Only after you have looked at this carefully and think that you can be successful should you play it.

DID IT!

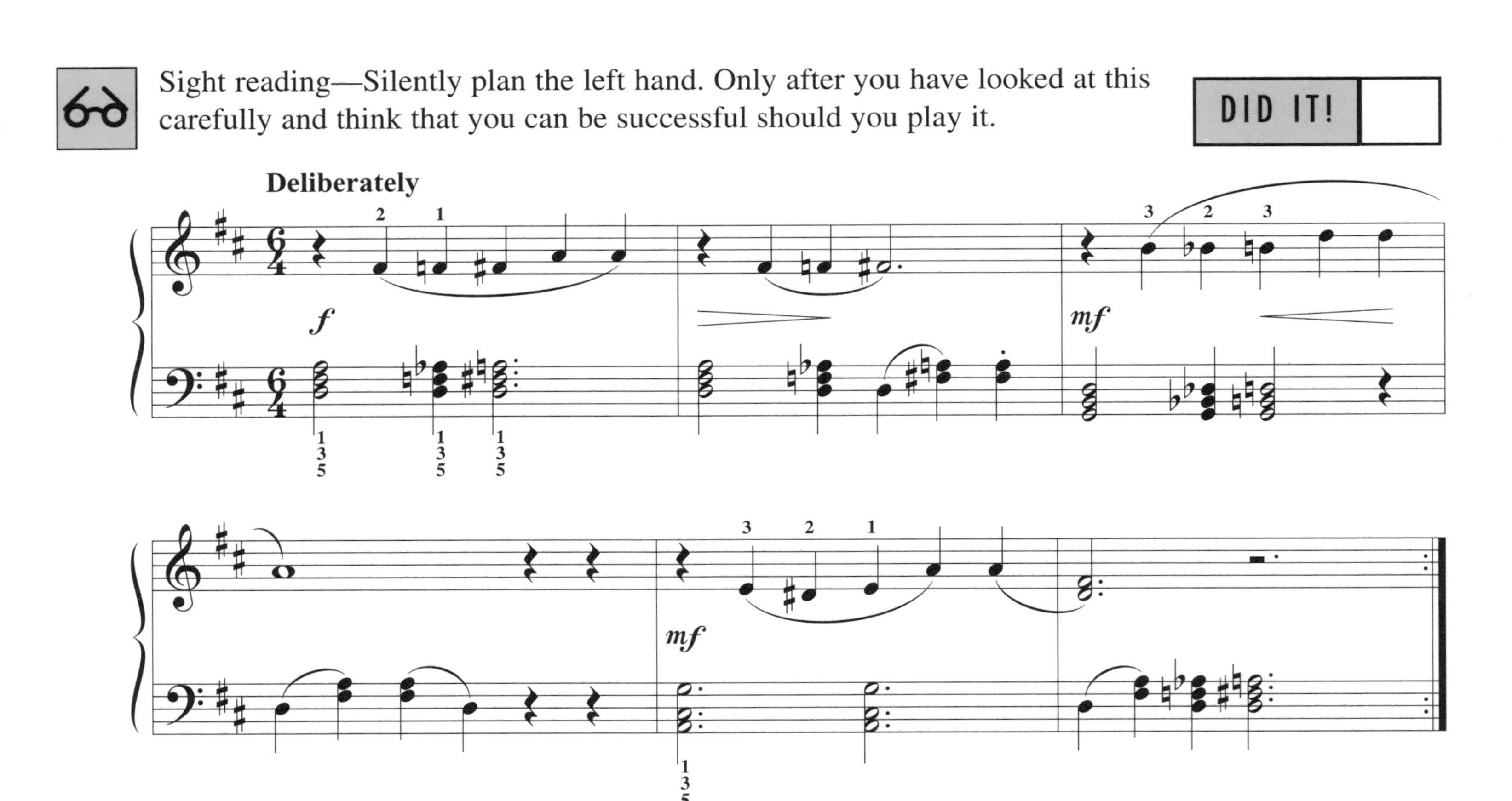

With 5 being the highest, how would you rate your sight reading? 1 2 3 4 5 (circle one)

Ensemble Piece

DID IT!

Before playing, plan the key and time signatures. Silently play on the top of the keys while counting aloud.

Barbershop Quartet

Teacher accompaniment (student plays as written)

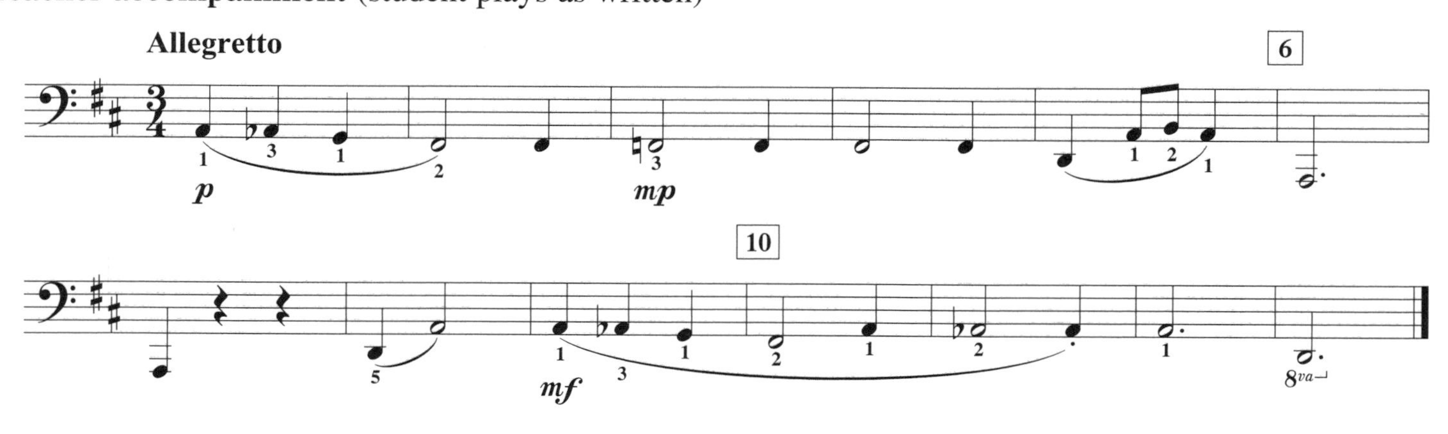

? After playing, ask yourself, "Did I play with a steady beat throughout?"

Unit 9

1
DAY ONE

New Concept: augmented triads in the keys of C, D, A, and E

Rhythm—Tap and count the following rhythm *pp*, fast, and evenly.

DID IT!

Interval Flash!—Block each group first. Then play as written.

DID IT!

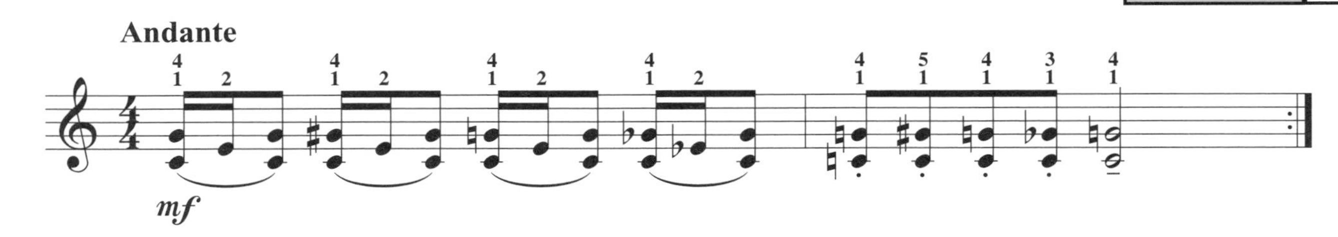

Sight reading—Play only the downbeats while looking at the entire score. Then the second time around, play *all* of the notes, always looking at the music and not at your hands.

DID IT!

Rhythm—Tap and count steadily, being sure to subdivide the dotted rhythms correctly.

DID IT!

Rhythm Flash!—Look at the first example for 10 seconds or less. Clap and count. Close the book and try it from memory! Then do the same for the second example.

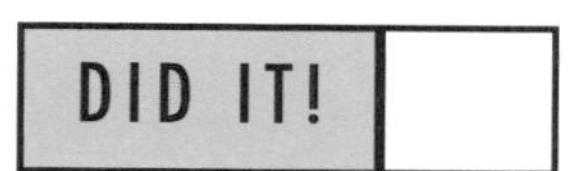

1. 

2. 

Sight reading—Play the melody of the harmonization. Then plan the left-hand chords. Prepare the piece hands together silently for one minute, and then play it!

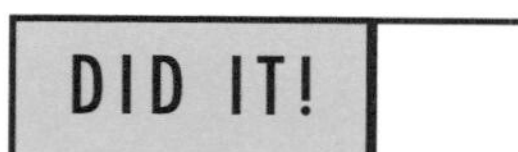

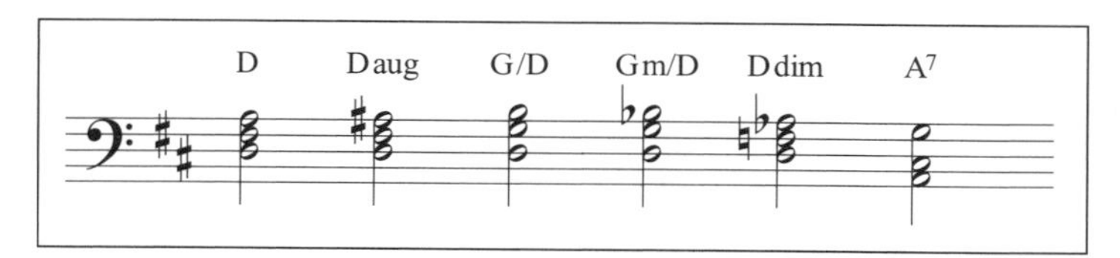

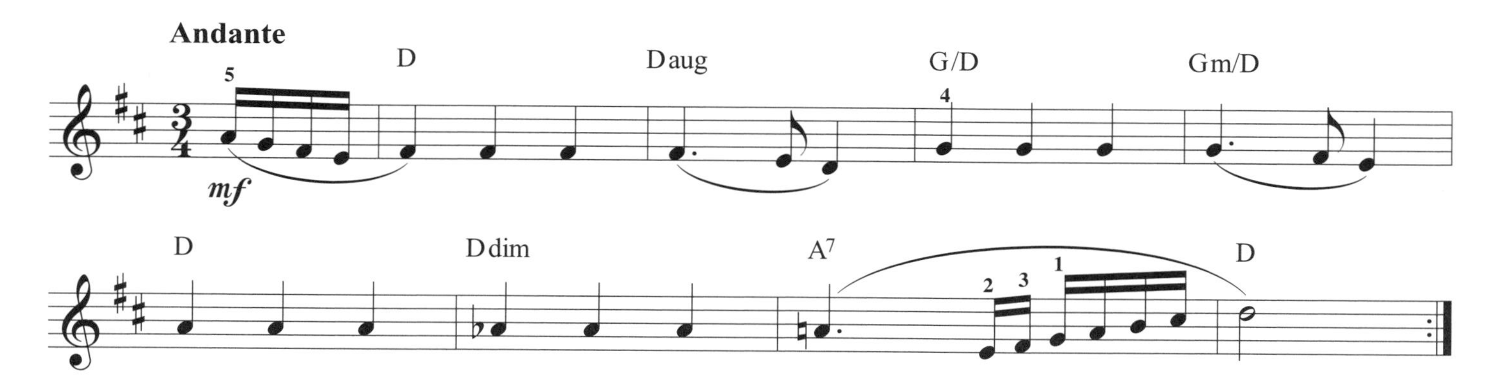

How would you rate your sight reading? excellent good so-so poor (circle one)

Rhythm—There is one mistake below. Find it, correct it, and then count it with energy in your voice!

DID IT!

Sight reading—Circle all of the diminished chords in the two examples below. Plan the rhythm and the fingering before you begin.

DID IT!

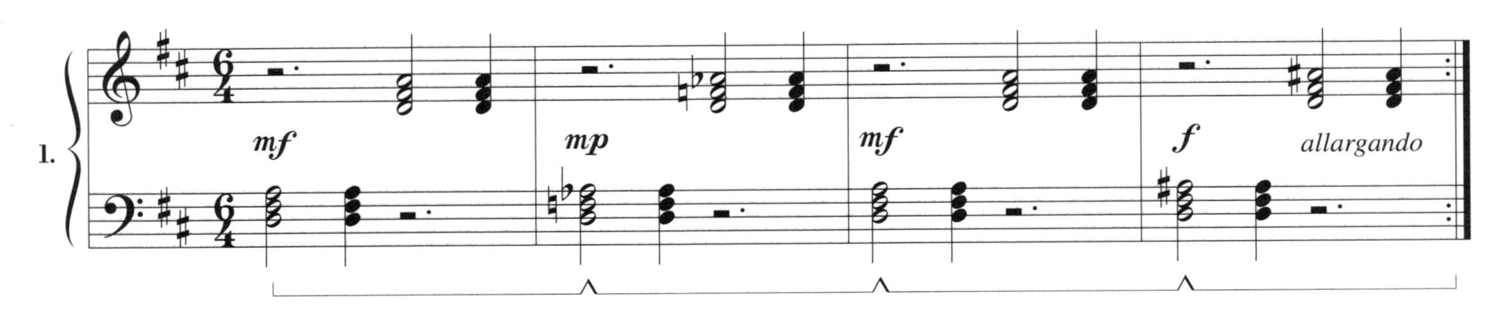

Sight reading—What is the difference between the two examples? Once you know, play them!

DID IT!

Rhythm—Tap the following rhythm. Whenever you see a "X," knock on the wood of the piano.

DID IT!

Rhythm Flash!—Plan each rhythm flash for ten seconds or less before clapping.

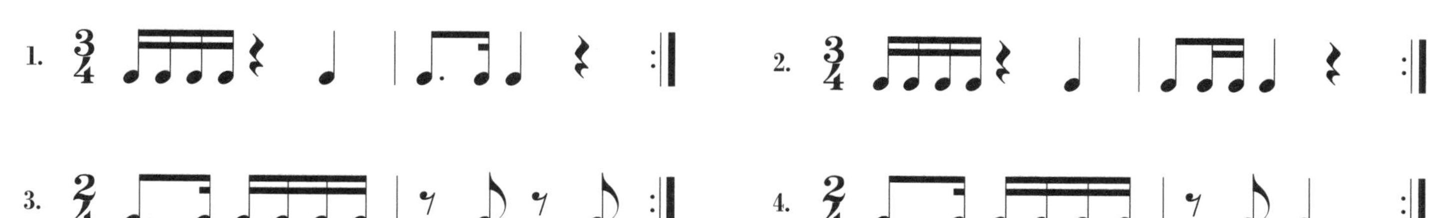

Sight reading—Observe the time and key signature. Decide which hand should play louder.

DID IT!

Transpose this piece to the following keys:

F major _____ D major _____

Rhythm—Set the metronome to a desired tempo. Tap and count with confidence!

DID IT!

Sight reading—Circle the diminished chord and place a square around the augmented chord. Plan the piece and then begin.

DID IT!

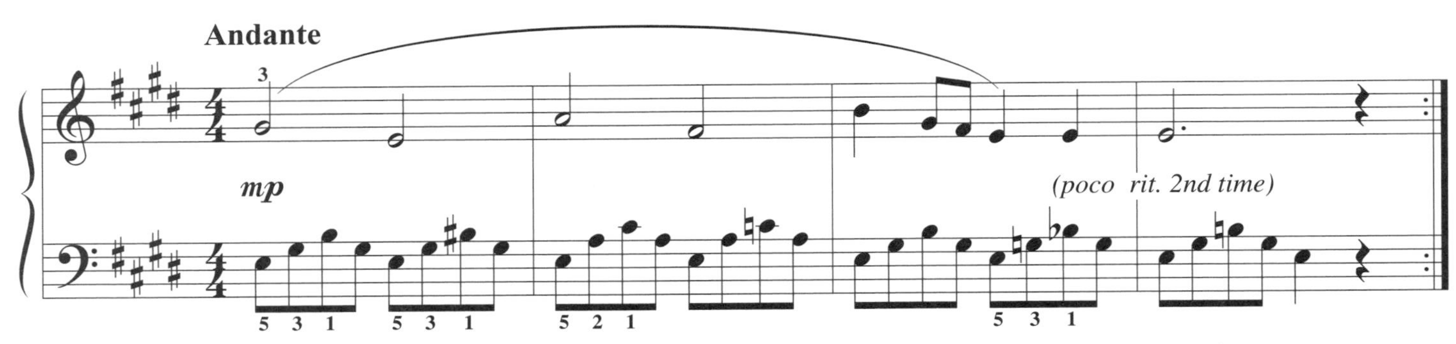

Sight reading—Play this piece without stopping. Always keep a steady beat and don't worry about mistakes!

DID IT!

Transpose this piece to two keys of your choice! _____ and _____ major.

Ensemble Piece

DID IT!

Before playing as written, block the left hand into chords. Then play the melody once through with the blocked chords.

Ode to Mozart

Teacher accompaniment (student plays as written)

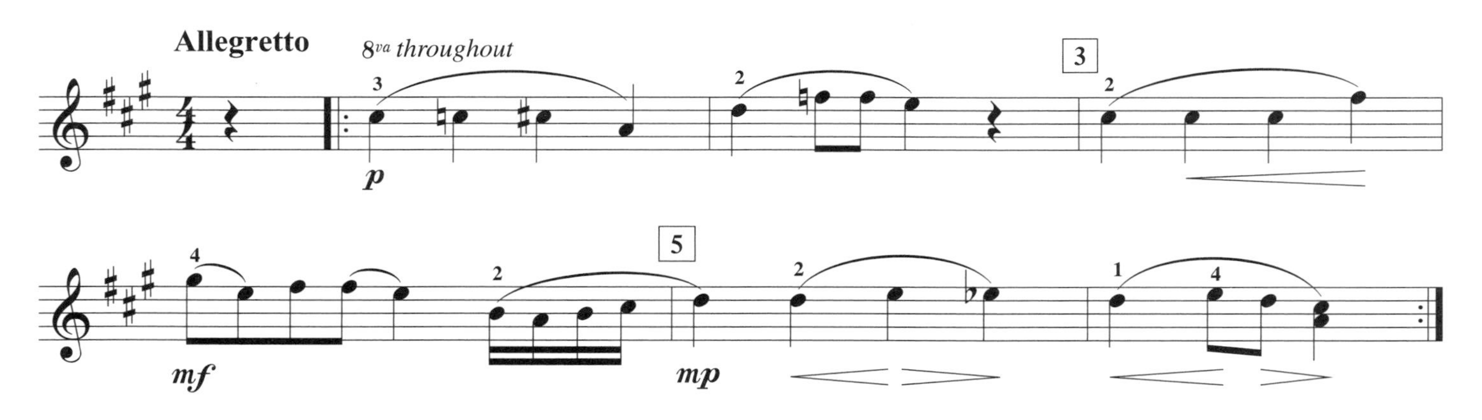

After playing, ask yourself, "Was I able to play from the beginning to the end while looking at the music and not my hands?"

Unit 10

1 DAY ONE

New Concept: pieces in the key of B minor.
Review of major and minor tonic triads;
changing clefs and ledger lines

Rhythm—Tap this rhythm as evenly as you can!

DID IT!

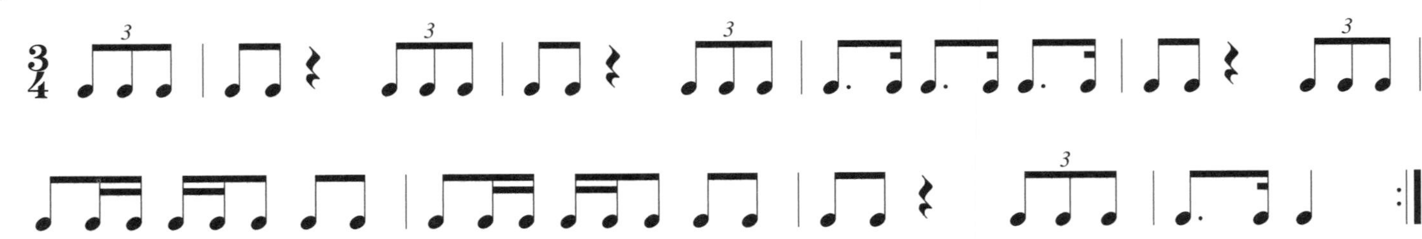

Interval Flash!—Label each pattern M (major), m (minor), + (augmented), or ∘ (diminished).

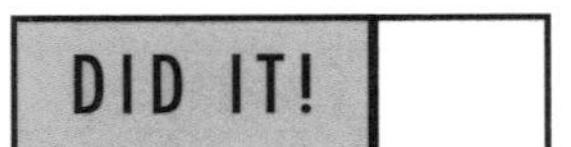

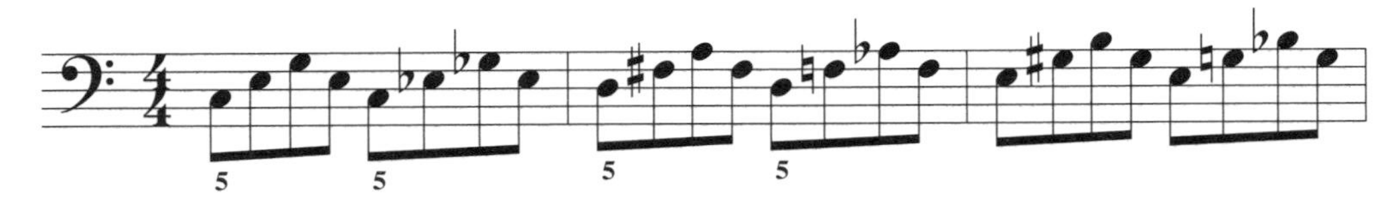

Continue the pattern in F, G, and A major.

Sight reading—Tap the rhythm hands together. Plan the key. Play the piece silently on top of the keys. Once you start, don't stop until the very end.

DID IT!

Transpose this piece to the keys of:

A minor _____ D minor _____

Rhythm—Tap and count with energy!

DID IT!

Rhythm Flash!—Plan carefully. Can you play the example once with the music and once without?

DID IT!

Sight reading—1. What do you notice about the rhythm of the 4 phrases in the right hand?
2. Set the metronome to ♩=92 and tap the rhythm.
3. Plan the left-hand chords.
4. Plan the scale passages.

DID IT!

Rhythm—Add the bar lines to the second line, then tap and count.

DID IT!

Chord Flash!—Move quickly to each new chord in order to plan it well before playing.

DID IT!

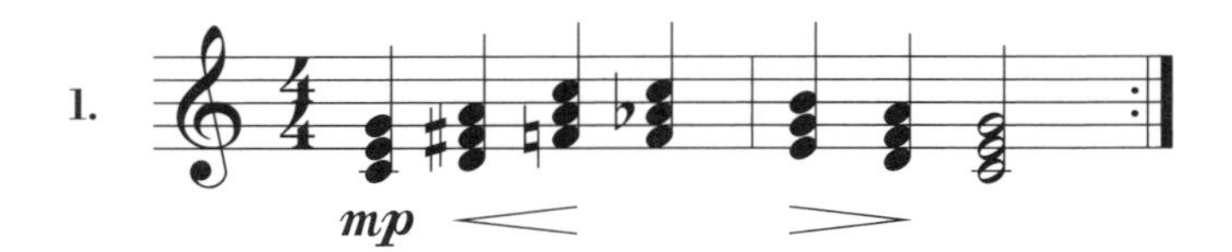

Sight reading—Plan the melody first. Then plan the left-hand chords. Remember to play a chord on every downbeat.

DID IT!

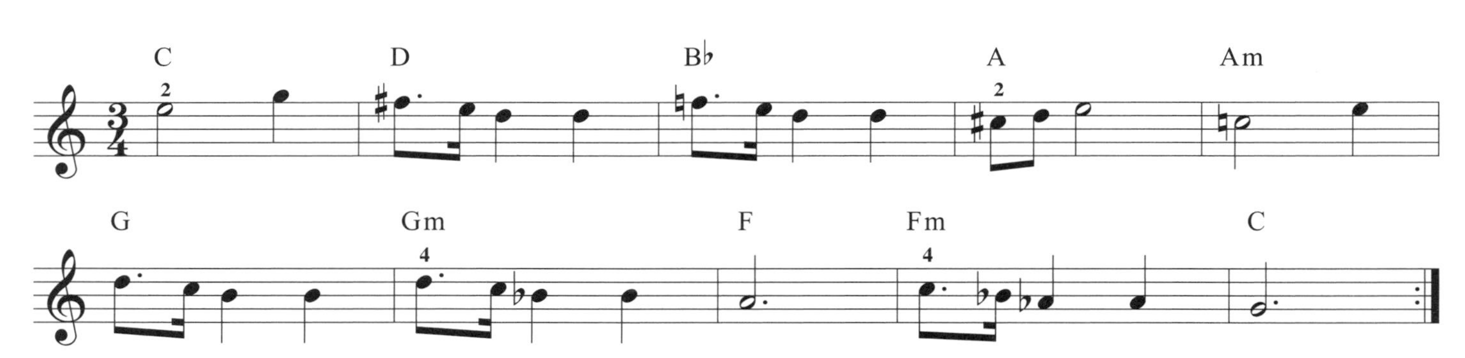

DAY FOUR

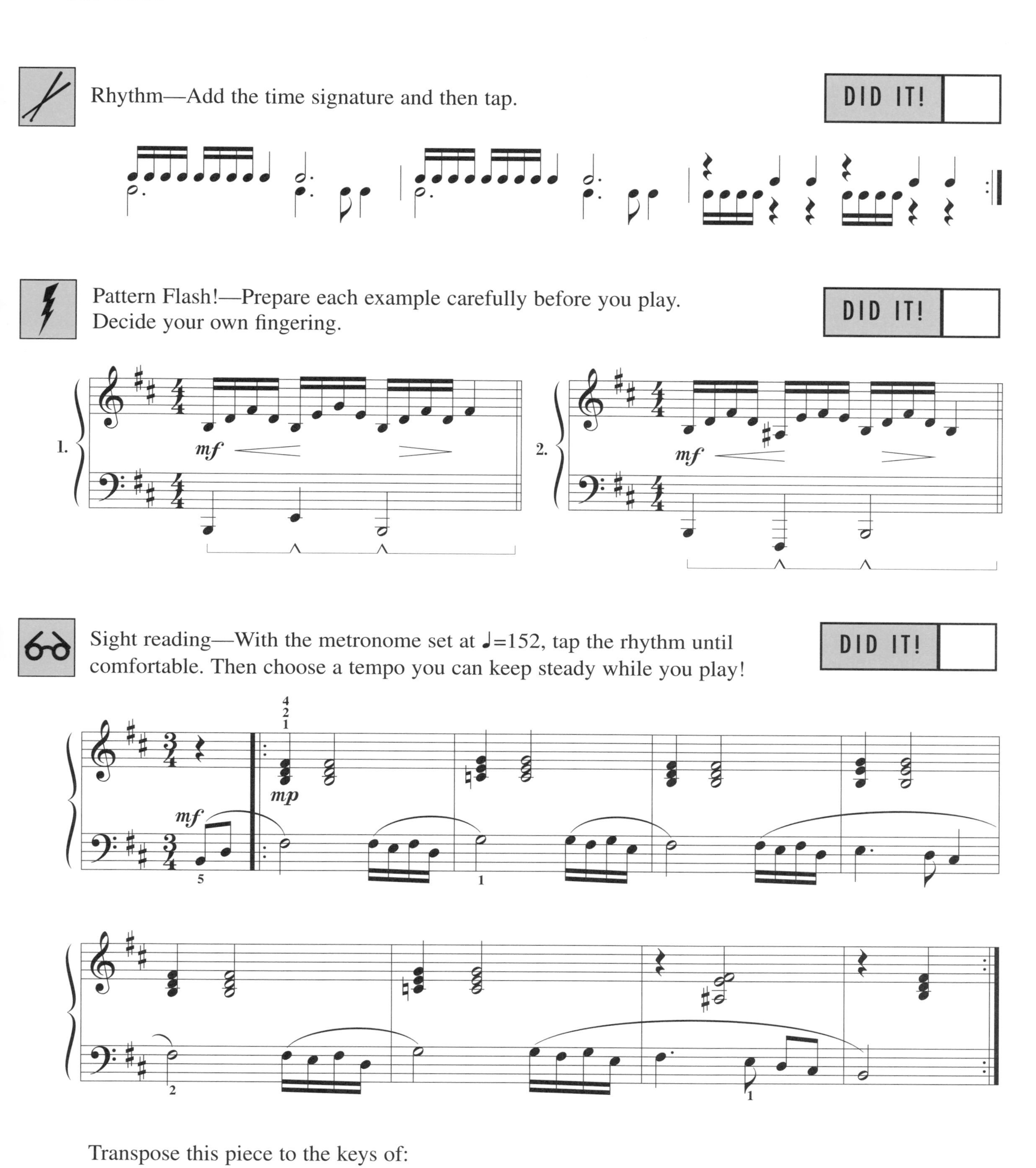

Rhythm—Add the time signature and then tap.

DID IT!

Pattern Flash!—Prepare each example carefully before you play. Decide your own fingering.

DID IT!

Sight reading—With the metronome set at ♩=152, tap the rhythm until comfortable. Then choose a tempo you can keep steady while you play!

DID IT!

Transpose this piece to the keys of:

D minor _____ A minor _____

Rhythm—*After* you clap this example, set the metronome to ♩=69, and notice how steady you were!

DID IT!

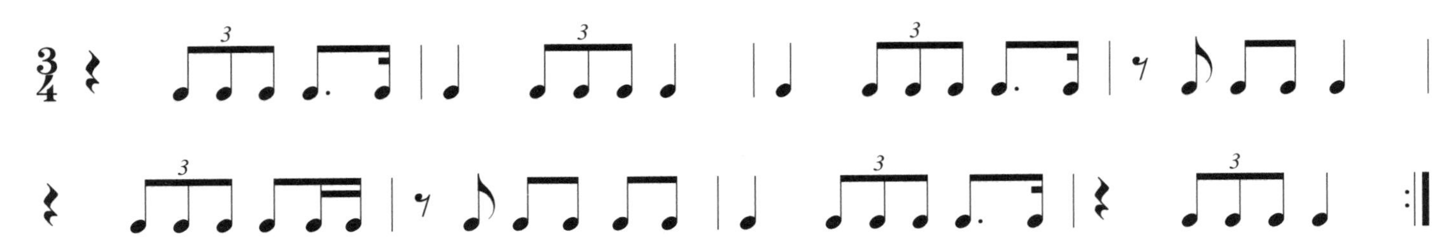

Sight reading—Plan the right hand chords carefully. Once you start, look at your music and not at your hands.

DID IT!

Sight reading—How are the patterns in each measure similar? Think the rhythm through before playing.

DID IT!

Ensemble Piece

DID IT!

Before playing as written, block the left-hand notes into chords. Observe the time and key signatures.

Song of the White Knight

Teacher accompaniment (student plays as written)

?

After playing, ask yourself, "Was I able to move with confidence to each left-hand pattern?"

Unit 11

1

DAY ONE

New Concept: harmonizations using chord symbols in the keys of A, D, and E minor

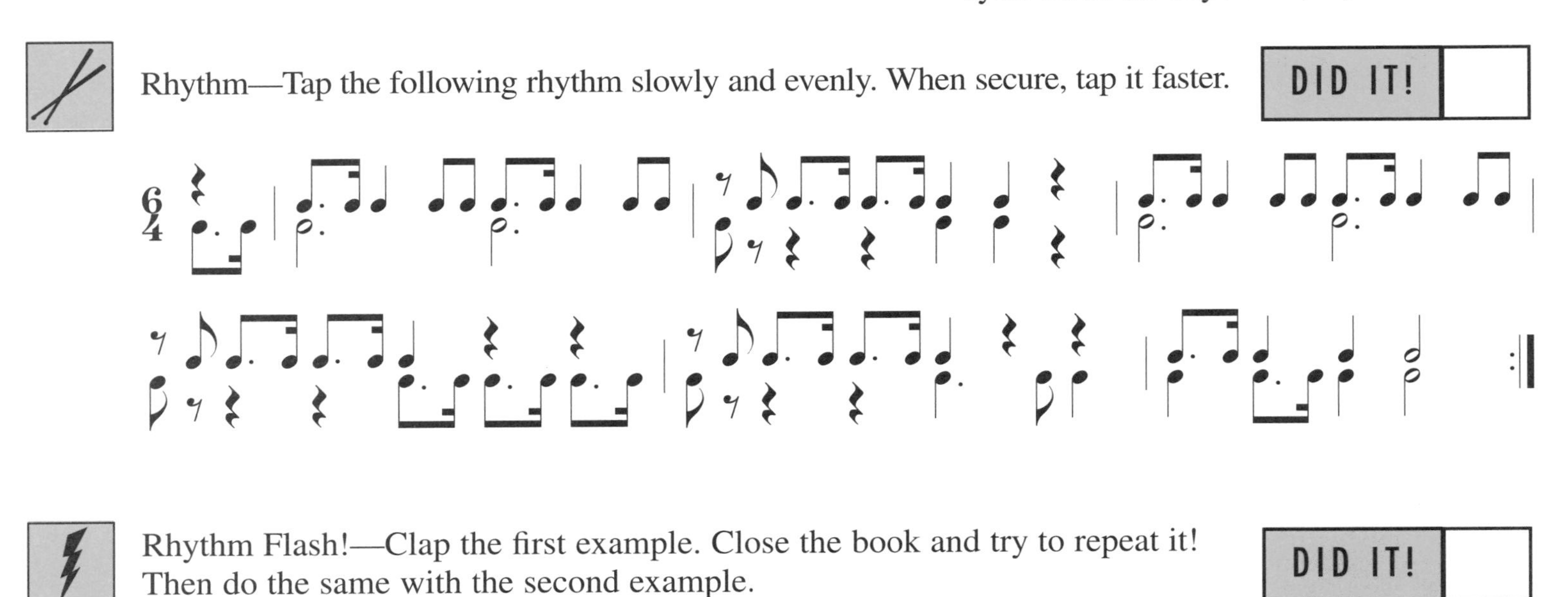

Rhythm—Tap the following rhythm slowly and evenly. When secure, tap it faster.

DID IT!

Rhythm Flash!—Clap the first example. Close the book and try to repeat it! Then do the same with the second example.

DID IT!

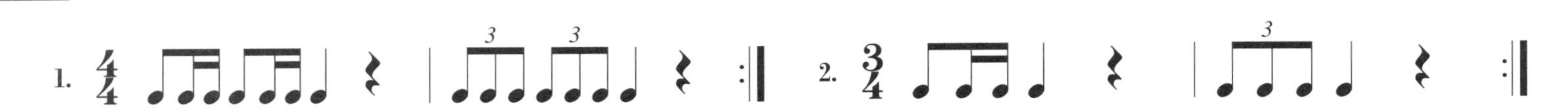

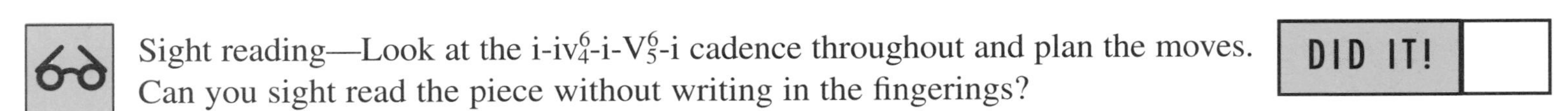

Sight reading—Look at the i-iv$^6_4$-i-V$^6_5$-i cadence throughout and plan the moves. Can you sight read the piece without writing in the fingerings?

DID IT!

Transpose this piece to the keys of:

E minor _____ D minor _____ C minor _____

Rhythm—Add the correct time signature to each example and tap with the metronome set at ♩=116.

DID IT!

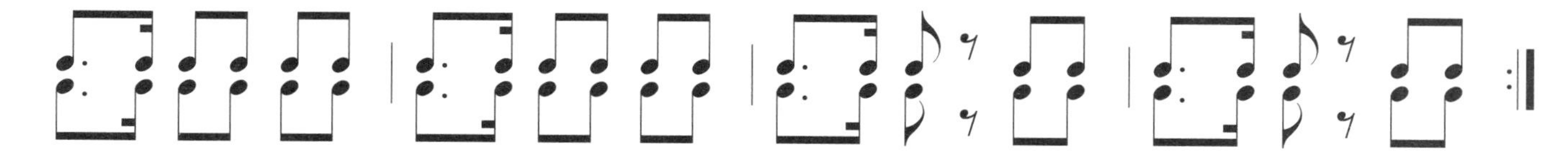

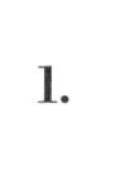

Pattern Flash!—Circle the iv_4^6 chord patterns and decide where the V_5^6 chords are as well.

DID IT!

Sight reading—Play the melody as beautifully and as *legato* as you can. Play the left hand more quietly than the right hand.

DID IT!

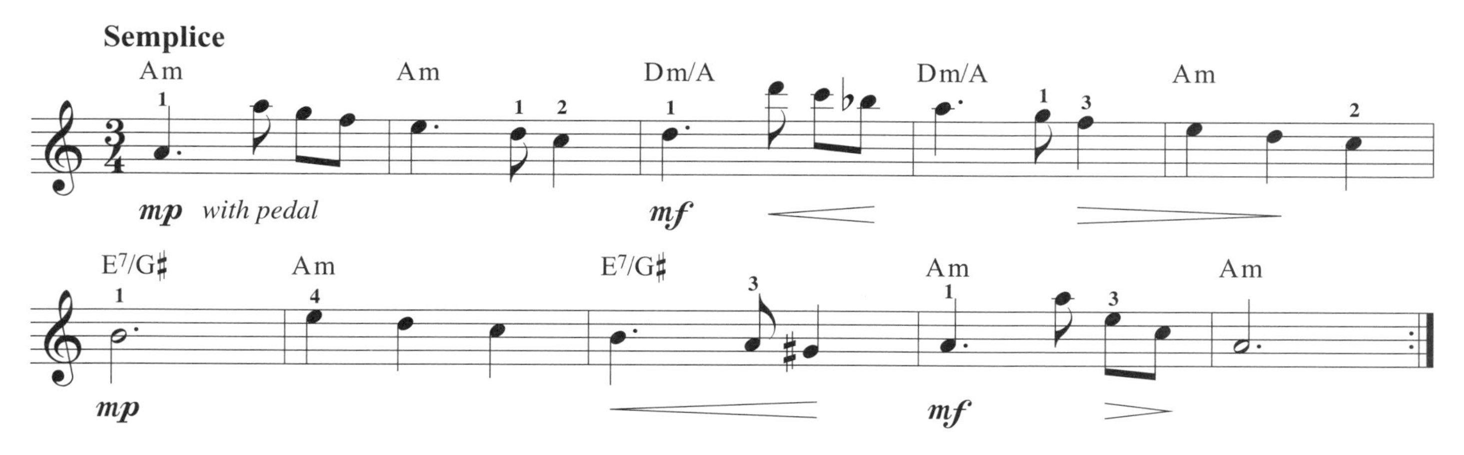

Rhythm—Clap this exercise. Every time you see an "X," knock on the wood of the piano. Count with confidence!

Sight reading—Play the right-hand melody. Then, prepare the chords in the left hand. Finally, play the piece hands together, with a chord on every downbeat.

DID IT!

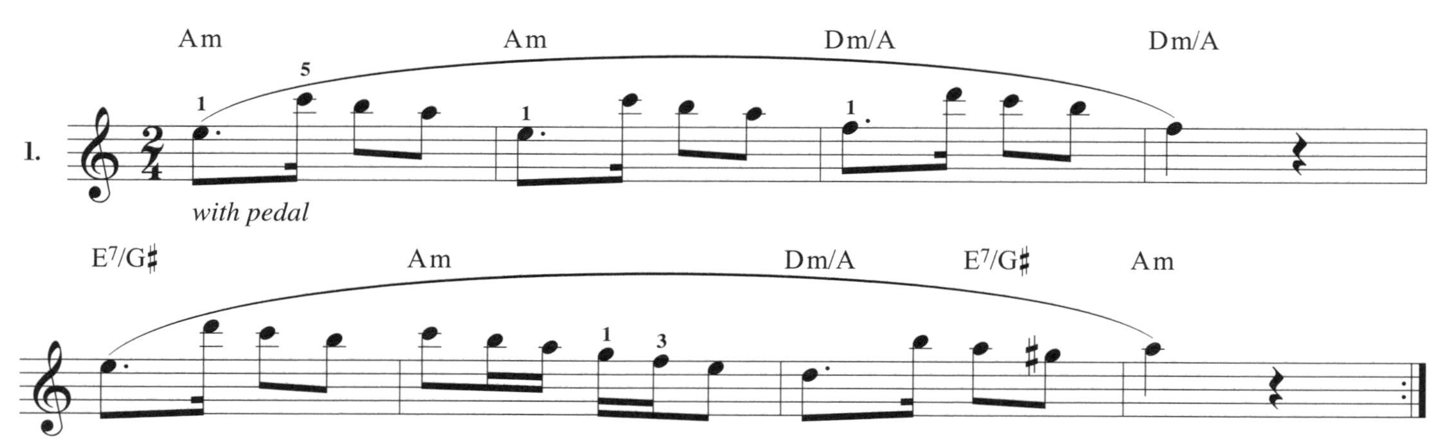

How is the next example similar to the previous example? Use your ear to figure out the left-hand chords.

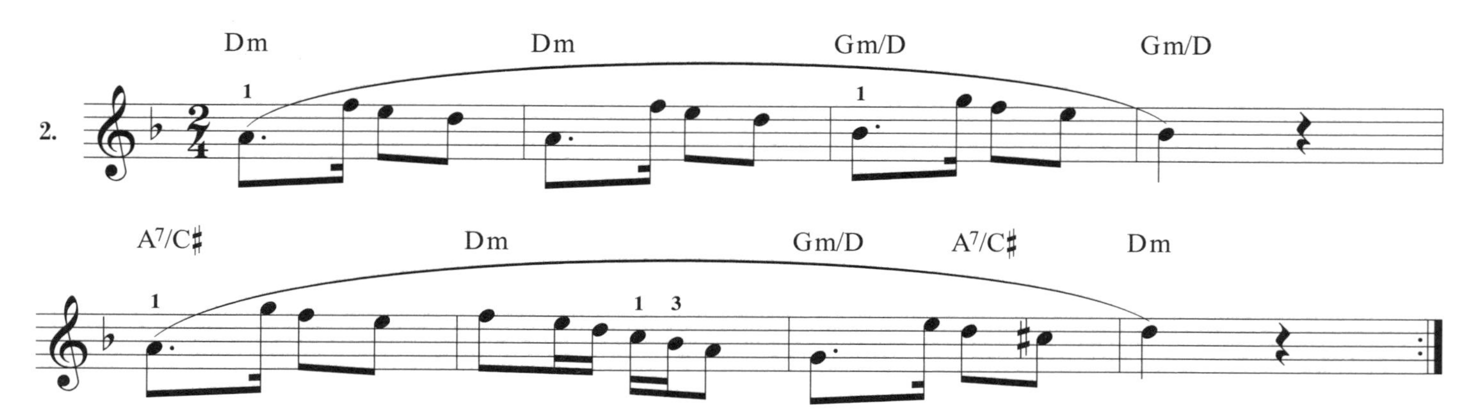

Chords for harmonization:

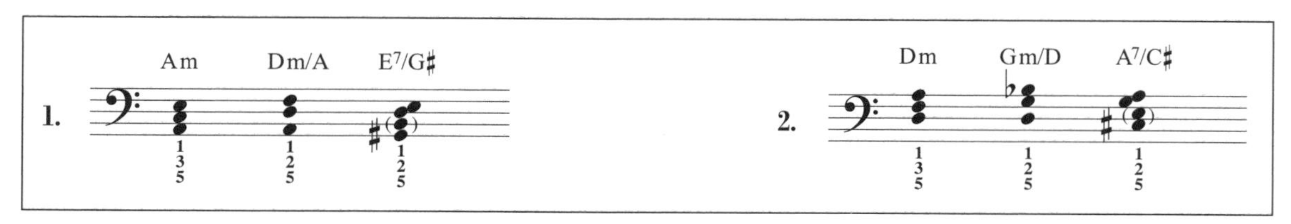

Rhythm—Add the bar lines. Set the metronome to ♩=100, and then clap and count aloud.

DID IT!

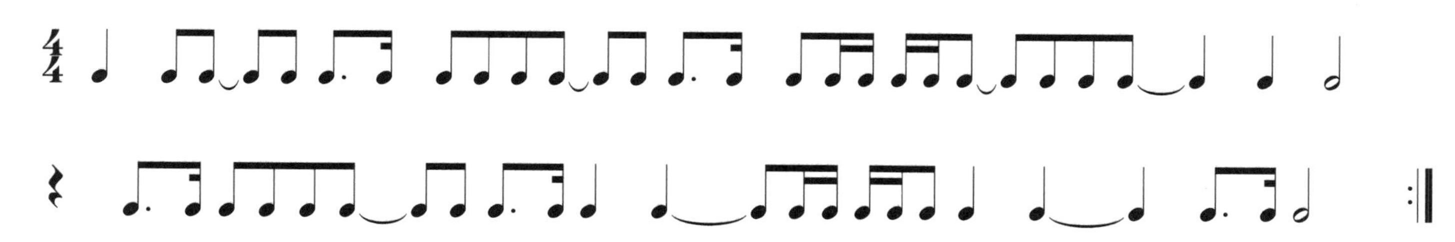

Pattern Flash!—Play the first pattern. Can you figure out the fingering? Close the book and try to play it again. Then do the same for the second example.

DID IT!

Sight reading—Plan the left-hand chords. Then play the right-hand melody. With hands together, play two chords per measure.

DID IT!

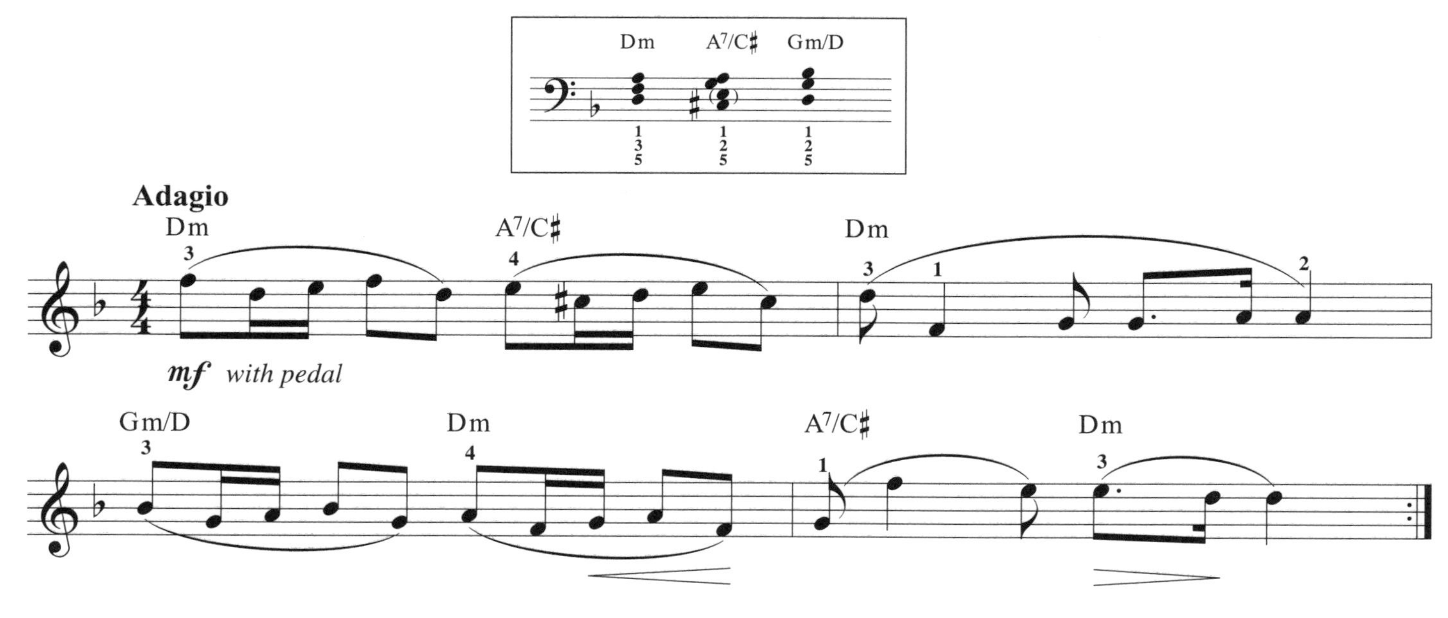

Rhythm—Clap this rhythm at two tempos of your choice. DID IT!

Rhythm—Complete each measure and then clap and count aloud evenly. DID IT!

Sight reading—Plan the right-hand melody and the left-hand chords. DID IT!

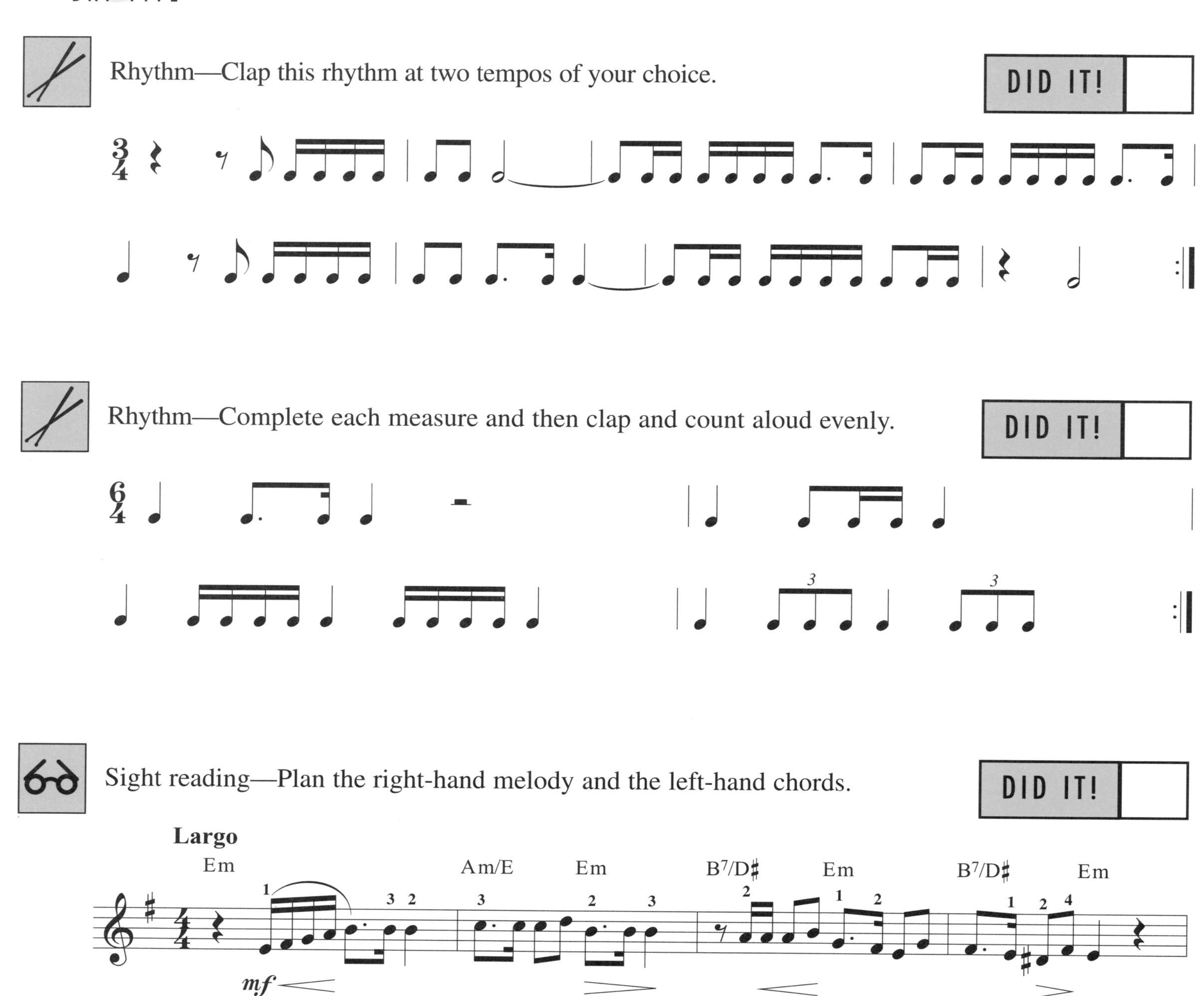

How was your sight reading of this challenging harmonization? Excellent Good Fair (circle one)

Ensemble Piece

DID IT!

The //// means to play the same ostinato pattern throughout the measure. Once you are secure with the 3 patterns, have your teacher play the melody.

Backup Guitar

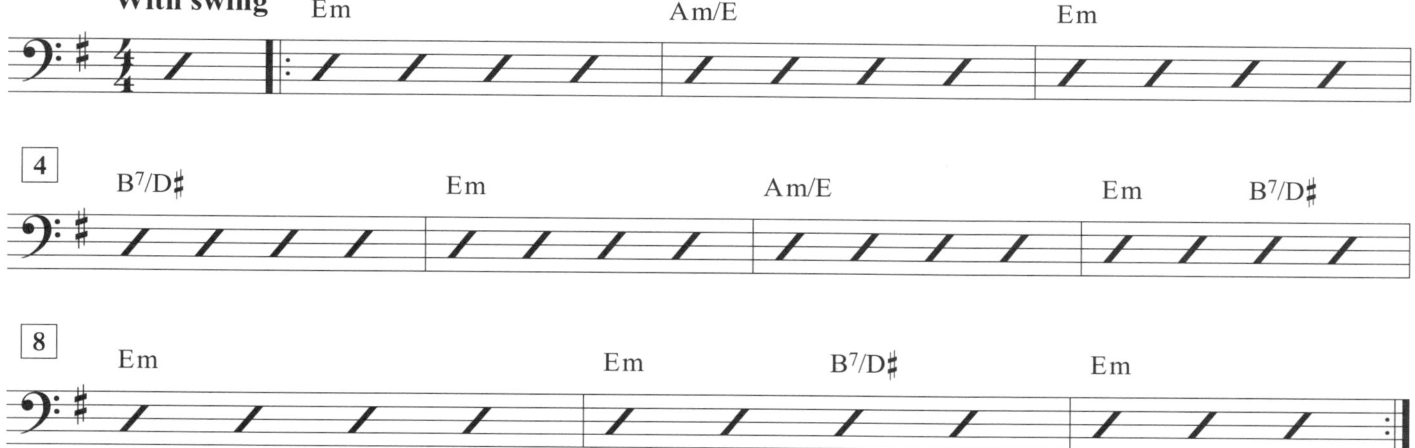

Teacher part (student plays as written)

? After playing, ask yourself, "Did I listen to the melody so that the accompaniment was quieter?"

Unit 12
Sight Reading and Rhythm Review

Plan both pieces before playing. When you think that you can play them successfully, play with confidence.

DID IT!

Minor Scales Flash—Which scales are which? Write "N" for natural minor. "H" for harmonic minor, and "M" for melodic minor. The first example has been done for you.

DID IT!

Minor Cadence Flash—How accurately can you play these patterns? Can you play them without fingering supplied?

DID IT!

Ledger Line Reading

DID IT!

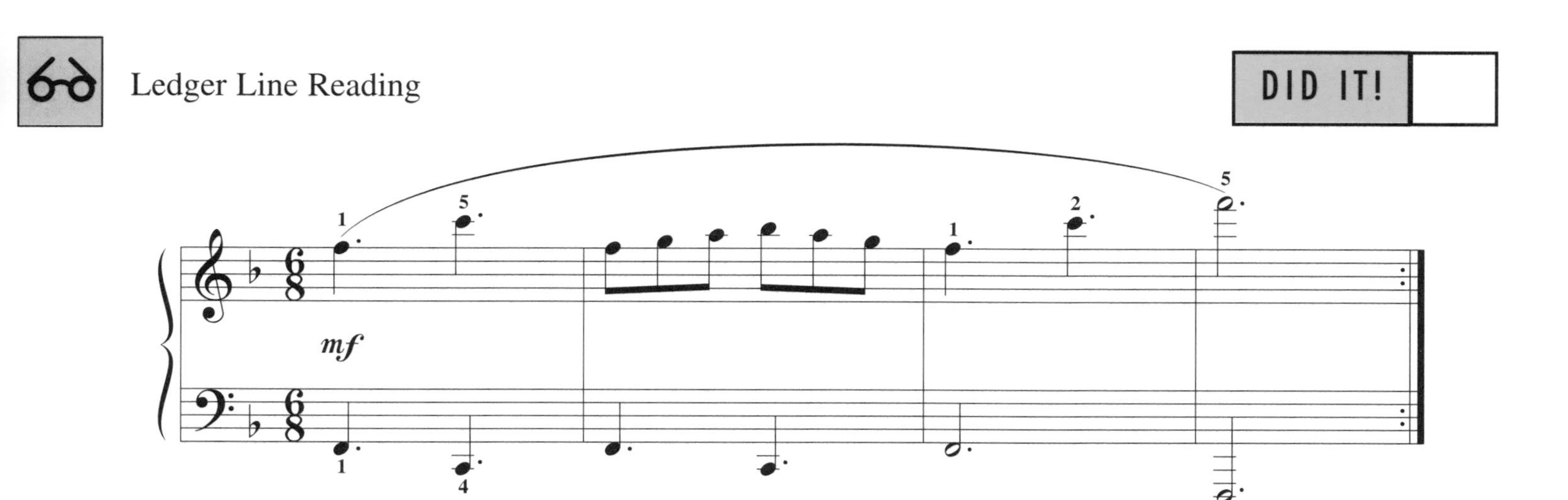

Rhythm—One measure in each example is incorrect. Find it, fix it, then clap the rhythm.

DID IT!

Interval Flash!—Circle the correct intervals. Then play each one slowly and surely. Prepare each interval before you play it.

DID IT!

Notice the similarities between all four examples. Use the first one as a guide for the other 3!

DID IT!

Cadence Flash—Look at each pattern very carefully before playing.

DID IT!

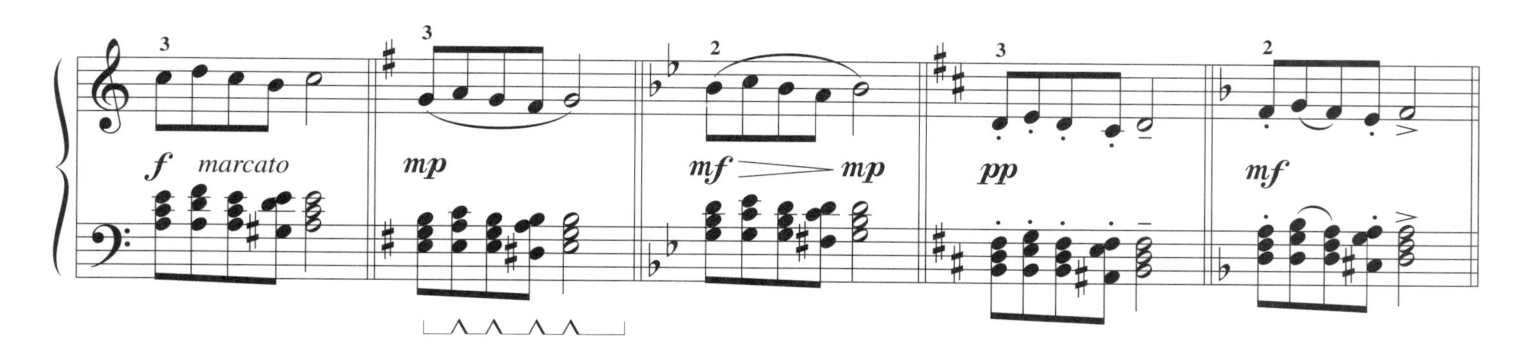

Sight reading—Silently play on the tops of the keys for accuracy.

DID IT!

Transpose to the keys of C minor and B minor.

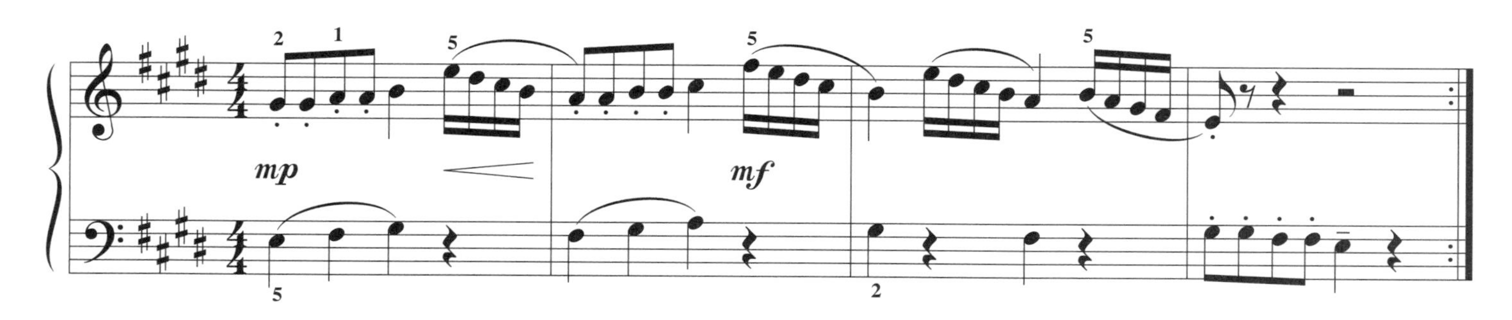

Transpose to the keys of D major and B major.

Harmonization in minor

Play hands apart until comfortable. Then try hands together.

DID IT!

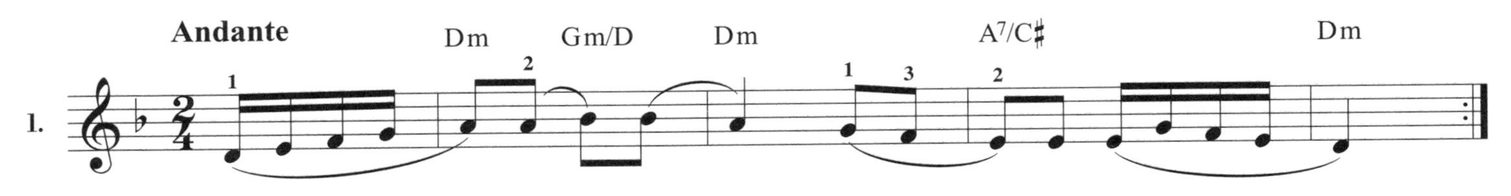

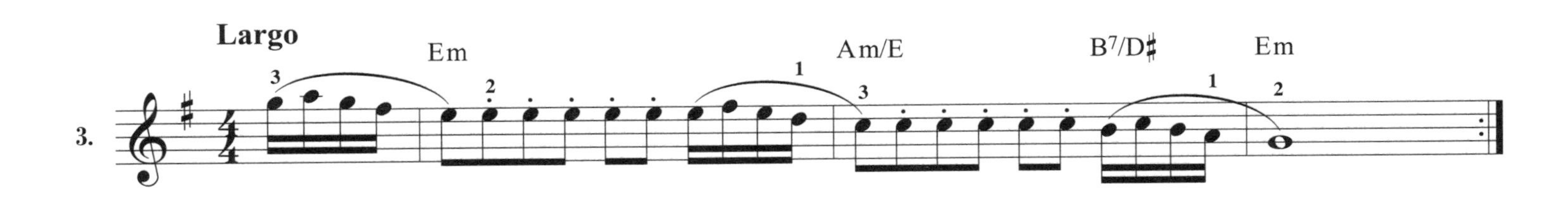

Chord Sight reading

In which measures does the right hand stay in the same place?

DID IT!

Analyze the chords. Where are the I, IV, and V chords? Decide the fingering.

Pattern Flash!—Look at each pattern for ten seconds or less. Then play them with confidence and don't stop!

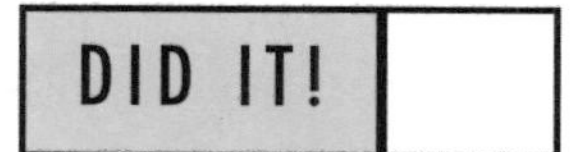

How was your sight reading? (circle one)

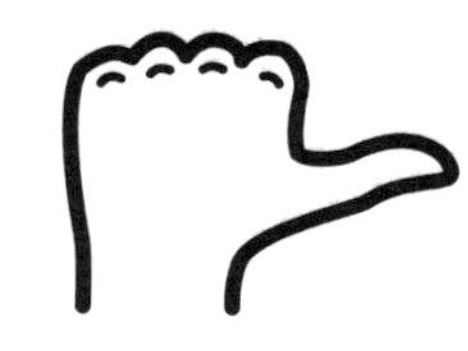

Certificate of Achievement

has successfully completed

SIGHT READING & RHYTHM EVERY DAY®
BOOK 6

of The FJH Pianist's Curriculum®

You are now ready for **Book 7**

Date

Teacher's Signature